Ivan Kushnir

Economy of Greenland

Series "Economy in countries"

first published: 2019
last updated: 2021-01-26

Ivan Kushnir. Economy of Greenland. Series "Economy in countries". - 2019. - 67 pages.

This book about the economy of Greenland from the 1970s to the 2010s. Source data from UN Data.

Size. In the 2010s, the gross domestic product of Greenland was equal to $2.7 billion per year; the value of agriculture was $461.9 million; the value of industry was $221.9 million. Since the share in the world is less than .01%, the country is classified as a micro economy.

Productivity. In the 2010s, the gross domestic product per capita was $48 556.4, the value of agriculture per capita was $8 176.1, the value of industry per capita was $3 927.8. Since the productivity is greater the average above average, the economy is classified as high developed.

Growth. In the 2010s, the growth of GDP was 1.4%; the growth of agriculture was 1.7%; the growth of industry was 4.2%.

Structure. In the 2010s, the economy of Greenland included: services (41.7%), agriculture (17.4%), transportation (12.3%), trade (10.4%), construction (9.8%), and industry (8.4%).

Exports and imports. In the 2010s, the imports were 44.1% higher than the exports, the net imports were equal to 17.1% of the GDP. The technological structure of exports are not better than the structure of imports.

Consumption and reproduction. The attitude of reproduction to the consumption is better than the global average, so the share of GDP in the world will increase.

Series "Economy in countries": parallel.page.link/en

ISBN: 9781795166324

Contents

Part I. Size

	The 2010s
GDP	$2.7 billion
The share in the world	0.0035%
Share in the Americas	0.011%
Share in Northern America	0.014%

Chapter I. Gross domestic product

The Greenlandic gross domestic product rose from $227.9 million per year in the 1970s to $2.7 billion per year in the 2010s, that is by $2.5 billion or 12.0 times. The change occurred at $2.2 billion due to a 4.8-fold increase in prices, as also at $303.9 million due to a 2.2-fold increase in productivity, as well as at $35.8 million due to the expansion in population. The average annual growth in gross domestic product is 2.7%. The minimum value of gross domestic product was in 1970 at $76.0 million. The maximum value of GDP was in 2018 at $3.1 billion.

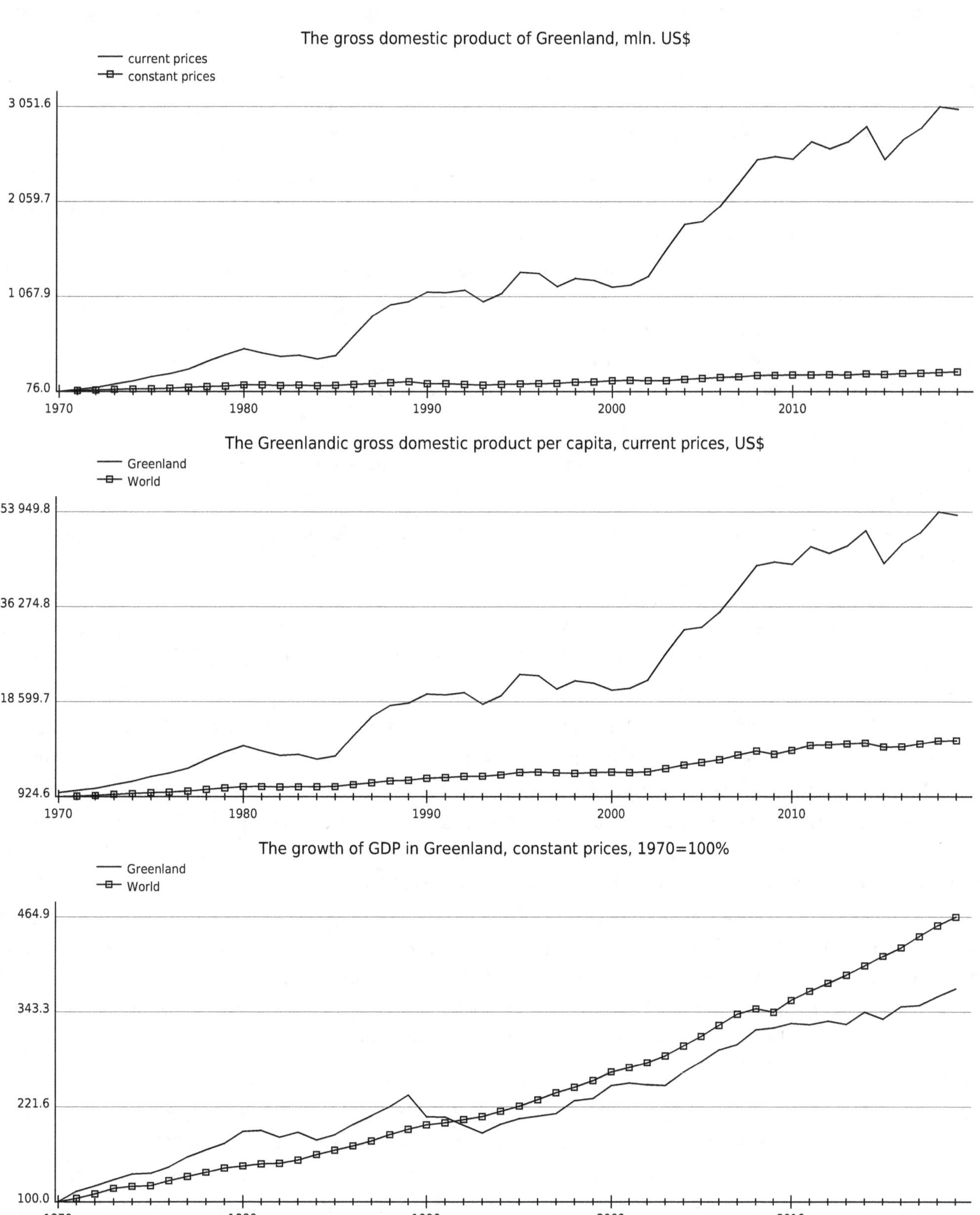

The 1970s

The gross domestic product of Greenland was $227.9 million per year in the 1970s, ranked 151st in the world. The share in the world was 0.0035%, and 0.010% in the Americas.

The gross domestic product of Greenland consisted of: household consumption expenditure (78.3%), capital formation (39.4%), and public expenditure (23.0%).

The Greenland's GDP per capita was $4 666.0 in the 1970s, ranked 33rd in the world. The Greenlandic gross domestic product per capita was greater than GDP per capita in the world ($1 620.8) in 2.9 times, and was greater than GDP per capita in the Americas ($4 044.6) by 15.4%.

The growth of GDP in Greenland was 6.4% in the 1970s, ranked 45th in the world, and was on a par with Algeria (6.4%), Qatar (6.4%), Iceland (6.4%). The growth of gross domestic product in Greenland (6.4%) was greater than growth of GDP in the world (4.1%), was greater than growth of GDP in the Americas (4.1%).

Comparison with neighbors. The gross domestic product of Greenland was less than in Canada ($166.4 billion) and in Iceland ($1.5 billion). The GDP per capita in Greenland was less than in Canada ($7.3 thousand) and in Iceland ($7.1 thousand). The growth of GDP in Greenland was greater than in Iceland (6.4%) and in Canada (4.2%).

Comparison with leaders. The gross domestic product of Greenland was less than in the United States ($1.7 trillion), in the USSR ($649.4 billion), in Japan ($558.0 billion), in Germany ($484.2 billion), and in France ($333.2 billion). The Greenland's gross domestic product per capita was greater than in the USSR ($2.6 thousand); but less than in the United States ($7.8 thousand), in France ($6.2 thousand), in Germany ($6.1 thousand), and in Japan ($5.0 thousand). The growth of gross domestic product in Greenland was greater than in the USSR (4.8%), in Japan (4.6%), in France (3.9%), in the USA (3.5%), and in Germany (3.1%).

The 1980s

The Greenland's GDP was $627.4 million per year in the 1980s, ranked 148th in the world. The share in the world was 0.0042%, and 0.012% in the Americas.

The GDP of Greenland included: household consumption expenditure (62.6%), public expenditure (42.6%), and capital formation (21.9%).

The Greenland's gross domestic product per capita was $11 886.7 in the 1980s, ranked 27th in the world, and was on a par with Belgium ($11.9 thousand), French Polynesia ($11.9 thousand), Austria ($12.1 thousand). The Greenlandic gross domestic product per capita was greater than GDP per capita in the world ($3 123.4) in 3.8 times, and was greater than GDP per capita in the Americas ($8 168.9) by 45.5%.

The growth of GDP in Greenland was 3.1% in the 1980s, ranked 84th in the world, and was on a par with the Caribbean (3.0%), Jordan (3.1%), Panama (3.1%). The growth of gross domestic product in Greenland (3.1%) was greater than growth of GDP in the world (3.0%), was greater than growth of gross domestic product in the Americas (2.8%).

Comparison with neighbors. The Greenland's gross domestic product was less than in Canada ($385.1 billion) and in Iceland ($4.0 billion). The GDP per capita in Greenland was less than in Iceland ($16.7 thousand) and in Canada ($15.0 thousand). The growth of GDP in Greenland was greater than in Canada (2.8%); but less than in Iceland (3.2%).

Comparison with leaders. The Greenlandic gross domestic product was less than in the United States ($4.2 trillion), in Japan ($1.8 trillion), in Germany ($990.0 billion), in the USSR ($887.0 billion), and in France ($729.5 billion). The GDP per capita in Greenland was greater than in the USSR ($3.2 thousand); but less than in the USA ($17.4 thousand), in Japan ($15.0 thousand), in France ($12.9 thousand), and in Germany ($12.7 thousand). The growth of gross domestic product in Greenland was greater than in France (2.3%) and in Germany (1.9%); but less than in the USSR (4.3%), in Japan (4.3%), and in the United States (3.1%).

The 1990s

The GDP of Greenland was $1.2 billion per year in the 1990s, ranked 167th in the world, and was on a par with Montenegro ($1.2 billion), the Central African Republic ($1.2 billion), Somalia ($1.2 billion). The share in the world was 0.0041%, and 0.012% in the Americas.

The GDP of Greenland consisted of: government expenditure (46.2%), household consumption expenditure (45.6%), and capital formation (19.7%).

The gross domestic product per capita in Greenland was $21 067.8 in the 1990s, ranked 27th in the world, and was on a par with Singapore ($20.9 thousand), Australia ($20.9 thousand), Canada ($21.3 thousand). The Greenland's GDP per capita was greater than GDP per capita in the world ($5 020.1) in 4.2 times, and was greater than gross domestic product per capita in the Americas ($12 984.7) by 62.3%.

The growth of gross domestic product in Greenland was -0.2% in the 1990s, ranked 173rd in the world. The growth of GDP in Greenland (-0.17%) was less than growth of GDP in the world (2.8%), was less than growth of gross domestic product in the Americas (3.1%).

Comparison with neighbors. The gross domestic product of Greenland was less than in Canada ($616.6 billion) and in Iceland ($7.3 billion). The gross domestic product per capita in Greenland was less than in Iceland ($27.3 thousand) and in Canada ($21.3 thousand). The growth of GDP in Greenland was less than in Iceland (2.4%) and in Canada (2.4%).

Comparison with leaders. The GDP of Greenland was less than in the United States ($7.6 trillion), in Japan ($4.3 trillion), in Germany ($2.2 trillion), in France ($1.4 trillion), and in the UK ($1.3 trillion). The Greenlandic gross domestic product per capita was less than in Japan ($34.3 thousand), in the USA ($28.7 thousand), in Germany ($27.0 thousand), in France ($24.1 thousand), and in the United Kingdom ($22.9 thousand). The growth of GDP in Greenland was less than in the USA (3.2%), in the UK (2.3%), in Germany (2.2%), in France (2.0%), and in Japan (1.5%).

The 2000s

The Greenlandic GDP was $1.8 billion per year in the 2000s, ranked 171st in the world. The share in the world was 0.0039%, and 0.011% in the Americas.

The gross domestic product of Greenland included: public expenditure (46.7%), household expenditure (44.7%), and capital formation (26.6%).

The Greenland's gross domestic product per capita was $32 018.6 in the 2000s, ranked 29th in the world. The Greenlandic gross domestic product per capita was greater than GDP per capita in the world ($7 176.3) in 4.5 times, and was greater than gross domestic product per capita in the Americas ($19 020.5) by 68.3%.

The growth of GDP in Greenland was 3.3% in the 2000s, ranked 124th in the world, and was on a par with South America (3.3%), Czechia (3.3%). The growth of GDP in Greenland (3.3%) was greater than growth of GDP in the world (3.0%), was greater than growth of GDP in the Americas (2.1%).

Comparison with neighbors. The GDP of Greenland was less than in Canada ($1.1 trillion) and in Iceland ($13.8 billion). The Greenlandic gross domestic product per capita was less than in Iceland ($46.8 thousand) and in Canada ($34.5 thousand). The growth of GDP in Greenland was greater than in Canada (2.1%); but less than in Iceland (3.5%).

Comparison with leaders. The Greenlandic gross domestic product was less than in the USA ($12.6 trillion), in Japan ($4.7 trillion), in Germany ($2.8 trillion), in China ($2.6 trillion), and in the UK ($2.3 trillion). The GDP per capita in Greenland was greater than in China ($1 954.1); but less than in the United States ($42.8 thousand), in the UK ($38.4 thousand), in Japan ($36.4 thousand), and in Germany ($34.0 thousand). The growth of gross domestic product in Greenland was greater than in the USA (1.9%), in the United Kingdom (1.7%), in Germany (0.73%), and in Japan (0.50%); but less than in China (10.3%).

The 2010s

The GDP of Greenland was $2.7 billion per year in the 2010s, ranked 172nd in the world, and was on a par with Burundi ($2.7 billion). The share in the world was 0.0035%, and 0.011% in the Americas.

The gross domestic product of Greenland consisted of: government consumption expenditure (44.9%), household consumption expenditure (39.8%), and capital formation (32.2%).

The Greenland's gross domestic product per capita was $48 556.4 in the 2010s, ranked 19th in the world, and was on a par with Austria ($48.5 thousand), Canada ($47.7 thousand), Finland ($47.7 thousand). The gross domestic product per capita in Greenland was greater than gross domestic product per capita in the world ($10 603.1) in 4.6 times, and was greater than GDP per capita in the Americas ($26 129.9) by 85.8%.

The growth of gross domestic product in Greenland was 1.4% in the 2010s, ranked 165th in the world, and was on a par with Samoa

(1.4%). The growth of GDP in Greenland (1.4%) was less than growth of GDP in the world (3.1%), was less than growth of gross domestic product in the Americas (2.2%).

Comparison with neighbors. The gross domestic product of Greenland was 622.9 times lower than in Canada ($1.7 trillion) and 6.9 times lower than in Iceland ($19.0 billion). The Greenlandic GDP per capita was 1.8% higher than in Canada ($47.7 thousand); but 15.6% lower than in Iceland ($57.5 thousand). The growth of GDP in Greenland was less than in Iceland (2.7%) and in Canada (2.2%).

Comparison with leaders. The gross domestic product of Greenland was 6 547.5 times lower than in the United States ($18.0 trillion), 3 829.8 times lower than in China ($10.5 trillion), 1 905.9 times lower than in Japan ($5.2 trillion), 1 334.8 times lower than in Germany ($3.7 trillion), and 1 008.5 times lower than in the UK ($2.8 trillion). The Greenlandic gross domestic product per capita was 8.5% higher than in Germany ($44.7 thousand), 15.1% higher than in the UK ($42.2 thousand), 18.8% higher than in Japan ($40.9 thousand), and 6.5 times higher than in China ($7.5 thousand); but 13.6% lower than in the USA ($56.2 thousand). The growth of GDP in Greenland was greater than in Japan (1.3%); but less than in China (7.7%), in the United States (2.3%), in Germany (1.9%), and in the UK (1.8%).

Chapter II. Value added

The value added of Greenland grew from $224.9 million per year in the 1970s to $2.7 billion per year in the 2010s, that is by $2.4 billion or 11.8 times. The change occurred at $2.1 billion due to a 5.1-fold increase in prices, as also at $259.4 million due to a 2.0-fold increase in productivity, as well as at $35.3 million due to the rise in population. The average annual growth in value added is 2.6%. The minimum value of value added was in 1970 at $75.0 million. The maximum value of value added was in 2018 at $2.9 billion.

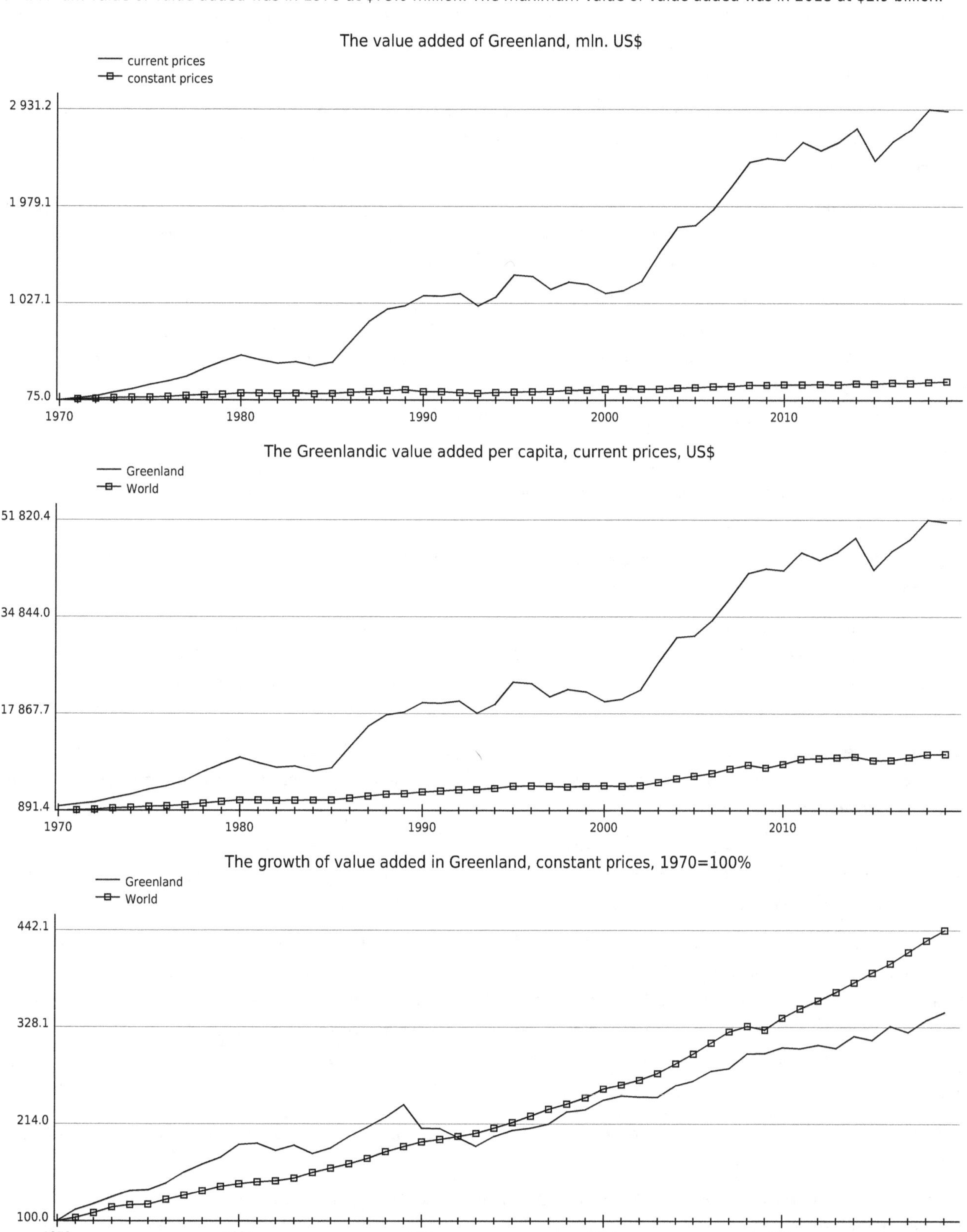

The 1970s

The Greenlandic value added was $224.9 million per year in the 1970s, ranked 150th in the world. The share in the world was 0.0036%, and 0.010% in the Americas.

The total value added of Greenland included: services (43.0%), agriculture (17.5%), transportation (12.6%), trade (11.5%), industry (10.4%), and construction (5.0%).

The value added per capita in Greenland was $4 606.4 in the 1970s, ranked 32nd in the world, and was on a par with Austria ($4.6 thousand). The Greenland's value added per capita was greater than value added per capita in the world ($1 564.4) in 2.9 times, and was greater than value added per capita in the Americas ($3 985.3) by 15.6%.

The growth of value added in Greenland was 6.4% in the 1970s, ranked 50th in the world, and was on a par with Honduras (6.4%), Yemen (6.4%), Grenada (6.5%). The growth of value added in Greenland (6.4%) was greater than growth of value added in the world (3.9%), was greater than growth of value added in the Americas (3.5%).

Comparison with neighbors. The value added of Greenland was less than in Canada ($155.4 billion) and in Iceland ($1.3 billion). The Greenland's value added per capita was less than in Canada ($6.8 thousand) and in Iceland ($6.2 thousand). The growth of value added in Greenland was greater than in Iceland (5.4%) and in Canada (3.8%).

Comparison with leaders. The value added of Greenland was less than in the United States ($1.7 trillion), in the USSR ($649.4 billion), in Japan ($545.3 billion), in Germany ($444.9 billion), and in France ($297.3 billion). The Greenland's value added per capita was greater than in the USSR ($2.6 thousand); but less than in the United States ($7.8 thousand), in Germany ($5.7 thousand), in France ($5.5 thousand), and in Japan ($4.9 thousand). The growth of value added in Greenland was greater than in Japan (4.9%), in the USSR (4.8%), in France (3.7%), in Germany (3.1%), and in the United States (2.9%).

The 1980s

The value added of Greenland was $619.4 million per year in the 1980s, ranked 148th in the world. The share in the world was 0.0042%, and 0.011% in the Americas.

The total value added of Greenland consisted of: services (43.0%), agriculture (17.5%), transportation (12.6%), trade (11.5%), industry (10.4%), and construction (5.0%).

The value added per capita in Greenland was $11 734.9 in the 1980s, ranked 23rd in the world, and was on a par with Northern Europe ($11.8 thousand), Germany ($11.6 thousand), Andorra ($11.6 thousand). The value added per capita in Greenland was greater than value added per capita in the world ($3 029.9) in 3.9 times, and was greater than value added per capita in the Americas ($8 159.2) by 43.8%.

The growth of value added in Greenland was 3.1% in the 1980s, ranked 83rd in the world, and was on a par with Chad (3.1%). The growth of value added in Greenland (3.1%) was greater than growth of value added in the world (2.9%), was greater than growth of value added in the Americas (2.7%).

Comparison with neighbors. The Greenland's value added was less than in Canada ($360.8 billion) and in Iceland ($3.5 billion). The value added per capita in Greenland was less than in Iceland ($14.7 thousand) and in Canada ($14.0 thousand). The growth of value added in Greenland was greater than in Canada (2.7%); but less than in Iceland (3.5%).

Comparison with leaders. The value added of Greenland was less than in the USA ($4.2 trillion), in Japan ($1.8 trillion), in Germany ($907.0 billion), in the USSR ($887.0 billion), and in France ($650.9 billion). The value added per capita in Greenland was greater than in Germany ($11.6 thousand), in France ($11.5 thousand), and in the USSR ($3.2 thousand); but less than in the United States ($17.4 thousand) and in Japan ($14.8 thousand). The growth of value added in Greenland was greater than in the United States (2.8%), in France (2.2%), and in Germany (2.0%); but less than in the USSR (4.3%) and in Japan (4.2%).

The 1990s

The Greenland's value added was $1.2 billion per year in the 1990s, ranked 167th in the world. The share in the world was 0.0042%, and 0.012% in the Americas.

The total value added of Greenland consisted of: services (42.9%), agriculture (17.5%), transportation (12.6%), trade (11.5%), industry (10.4%), and construction (5.0%).

The value added per capita in Greenland was $20 780.8 in the 1990s, ranked 24th in the world, and was on a par with Northern Europe ($20.8 thousand), Finland ($21.1 thousand), Hong Kong ($21.3 thousand). The Greenlandic value added per capita was greater than value added per capita in the world ($4 799.9) in 4.3 times, and was greater than value added per capita in the Americas ($12 777.9) by 62.6%.

The growth of value added in Greenland was -0.2% in the 1990s, ranked 172nd in the world. The growth of value added in Greenland (-0.24%) was less than growth of value added in the world (2.7%), was less than growth of value added in the Americas (2.8%).

Comparison with neighbors. The Greenlandic value added was less than in Canada ($571.5 billion) and in Iceland ($6.4 billion). The Greenlandic value added per capita was greater than in Canada ($19.7 thousand); but less than in Iceland ($24.0 thousand). The growth of value added in Greenland was less than in Iceland (2.8%) and in Canada (2.3%).

Comparison with leaders. The Greenland's value added was less than in the United States ($7.6 trillion), in Japan ($4.3 trillion), in Germany ($2.0 trillion), in France ($1.3 trillion), and in the United Kingdom ($1.2 trillion). The Greenland's value added per capita was less than in Japan ($34.2 thousand), in the United States ($28.6 thousand), in Germany ($24.5 thousand), in France ($21.6 thousand), and in the United Kingdom ($21.4 thousand). The growth of value added in Greenland was less than in the USA (2.8%), in the UK (2.4%), in Germany (2.1%), in France (1.8%), and in Japan (1.8%).

The 2000s

The value added of Greenland was $1.8 billion per year in the 2000s, ranked 170th in the world, and was on a par with San Marino ($1.8 billion). The share in the world was 0.0040%, and 0.011% in the Americas.

The total value added of Greenland included: services (43.2%), agriculture (16.1%), transportation (13.1%), trade (10.6%), industry (10.3%), and construction (6.7%).

The value added per capita in Greenland was $31 026.6 in the 2000s, ranked 27th in the world, and was on a par with Belgium ($31.2 thousand), Australasia ($30.7 thousand), Germany ($30.7 thousand). The value added per capita in Greenland was greater than value added per capita in the world ($6 818.0) in 4.6 times, and was greater than value added per capita in the Americas ($18 623.4) by 66.6%.

The growth of value added in Greenland was 2.6% in the 2000s, ranked 143rd in the world, and was on a par with Macedonia (2.5%), New Zealand (2.5%). The growth of value added in Greenland (2.6%) was less than growth of value added in the world (2.9%), was greater than growth of value added in the Americas (1.9%).

Comparison with neighbors. The Greenlandic value added was less than in Canada ($1.0 trillion) and in Iceland ($12.1 billion). The Greenlandic value added per capita was less than in Iceland ($40.8 thousand) and in Canada ($32.1 thousand). The growth of value added in Greenland was greater than in Canada (2.1%); but less than in Iceland (2.8%).

Comparison with leaders. The Greenlandic value added was less than in the USA ($12.6 trillion), in Japan ($4.7 trillion), in China ($2.6 trillion), in Germany ($2.5 trillion), and in the UK ($2.1 trillion). The value added per capita in Greenland was greater than in Germany ($30.7 thousand) and in China ($1 954.1); but less than in the United States ($42.8 thousand), in Japan ($36.4 thousand), and in the UK ($34.6 thousand). The growth of value added in Greenland was greater than in the United States (1.7%), in the UK (1.7%), in Germany (0.65%), and in Japan (0.27%); but less than in China (10.2%).

The 2010s

The Greenland's value added was $2.7 billion per year in the 2010s, ranked 172nd in the world. The share in the world was 0.0036%, and 0.011% in the Americas.

The total value added of Greenland included: services (41.7%), agriculture (17.4%), transportation (12.3%), trade (10.4%), construction (9.8%), and industry (8.4%).

The value added per capita in Greenland was $46 957.8 in the 2010s, ranked 18th in the world. The Greenland's value added per capita was greater than value added per capita in the world ($10 094.6) in 4.7 times, and was greater than value added per capita in the Americas ($25 411.8) by 84.8%.

The growth of value added in Greenland was 1.5% in the 2010s, ranked 164th in the world. The growth of value added in Greenland (1.5%) was less than growth of value added in the world (3.1%), was less than growth of value added in the Americas (2.1%).

Comparison with neighbors. The Greenland's value added was 601.9 times lower than in Canada ($1.6 trillion) and 6.4 times lower than in Iceland ($16.9 billion). The Greenlandic value added per capita was 5.3% higher than in Canada ($44.6 thousand); but 8.6% lower than in Iceland ($51.4 thousand). The growth of value added in Greenland was less than in Iceland (3.0%) and in Canada (2.4%).

Comparison with leaders. The value added of Greenland was 6 770.5 times lower than in the United States ($18.0 trillion), 3 960.2 times lower than in China ($10.5 trillion), 1 960.7 times lower than in Japan ($5.2 trillion), 1 244.9 times lower than in Germany ($3.3 trillion), and 931.2 times lower than in the UK ($2.5 trillion). The value added per capita in Greenland was 15.5% higher than in Japan ($40.7 thousand), 16.4% higher than in Germany ($40.3 thousand), 24.7% higher than in the UK ($37.7 thousand), and 6.3 times higher than in China ($7.5 thousand); but 16.5% lower than in the USA ($56.2 thousand). The growth of value added in Greenland was greater than in Japan (1.3%); but less than in China (7.7%), in the United States (2.2%), in Germany (1.9%), and in the UK (1.8%).

Chapter III. Gross national income

The Greenland's GNI grew from $205.4 million per year in the 1970s to $2.7 billion per year in the 2010s, that is by $2.5 billion or 13.0 times. The change occurred at $2.1 billion due to a 4.8-fold increase in prices, as also at $314.5 million due to a 2.3-fold increase in productivity, as well as at $32.2 million due to the growing in population. The average annual growth in gross national income is 2.9%. The minimum value of gross national income was in 1970 at $68.5 million. The maximum value of gross national income was in 2018 at $3.0 billion.

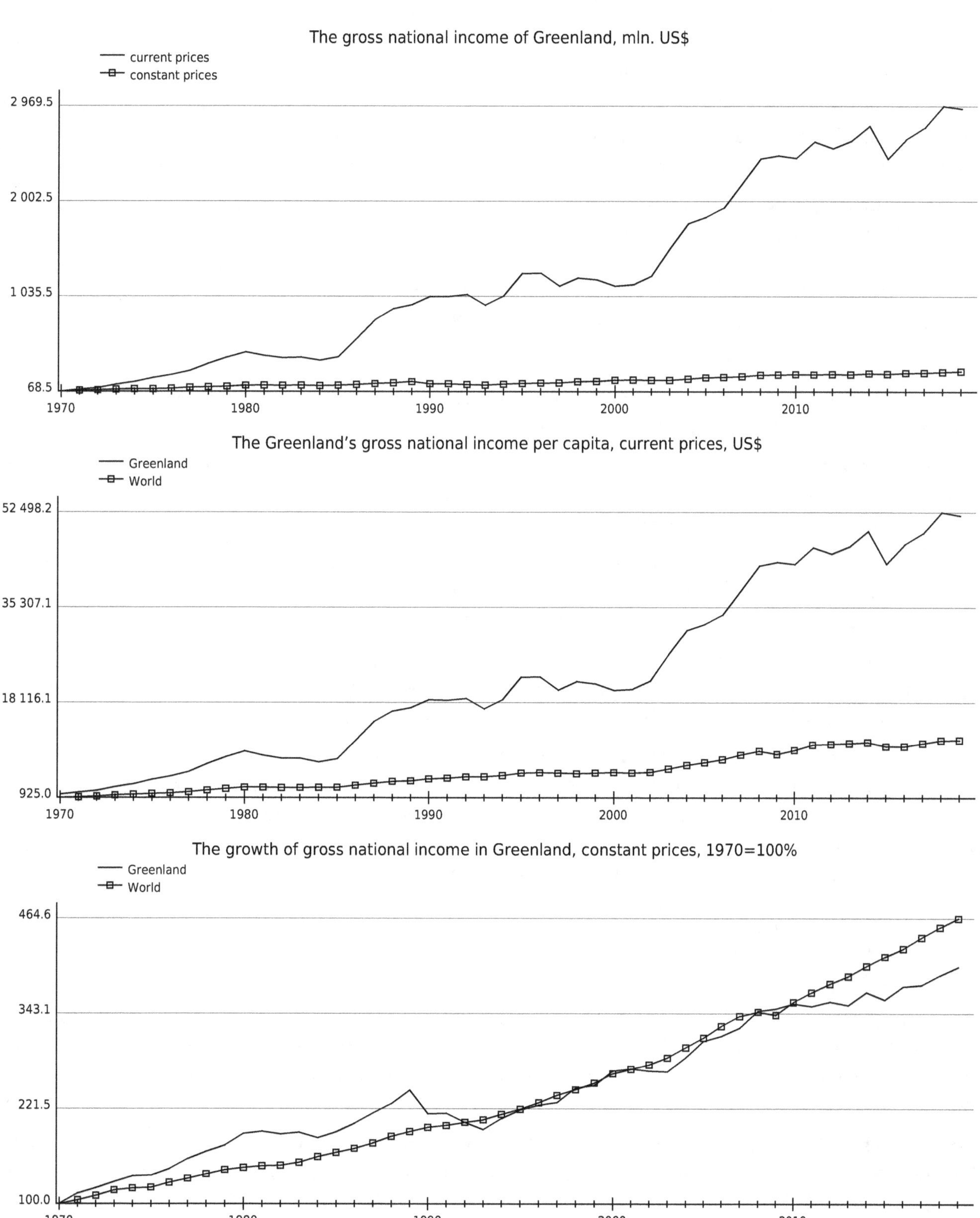

The 1970s

The Greenlandic gross national income was $205.4 million per year in the 1970s, ranked 152nd in the world. The share in the world was 0.0031%, and 0.0091% in the Americas.

The GNI per capita in Greenland was $4 206.4 in the 1970s, ranked 36th in the world, and was on a par with Nauru ($4.3 thousand), New Zealand ($4.3 thousand), Aruba ($4.1 thousand). The GNI per capita in Greenland was greater than GNI per capita in the world ($1 624.3) in 2.6 times, and was greater than gross national income per capita in the Americas ($4 019.9) by 4.6%.

The growth of GNI in Greenland was 6.4% in the 1970s, ranked 48th in the world, and was on a par with Algeria (6.4%), Myanmar (6.4%), Saint Lucia (6.4%). The growth of GNI in Greenland (6.4%) was greater than growth of gross national income in the world (4.1%), was greater than growth of GNI in the Americas (4.0%).

Comparison with neighbors. The gross national income of Greenland was less than in Canada ($162.0 billion) and in Iceland ($1.5 billion). The Greenlandic GNI per capita was less than in Canada ($7.1 thousand) and in Iceland ($7.0 thousand). The growth of gross national income in Greenland was greater than in Iceland (6.2%) and in Canada (4.1%).

Comparison with leaders. The Greenlandic GNI was less than in the USA ($1.7 trillion), in the USSR ($649.4 billion), in Japan ($558.5 billion), in Germany ($486.2 billion), and in France ($334.3 billion). The Greenland's gross national income per capita was greater than in the USSR ($2.6 thousand); but less than in the United States ($7.8 thousand), in France ($6.2 thousand), in Germany ($6.2 thousand), and in Japan ($5.0 thousand). The growth of gross national income in Greenland was greater than in the USSR (4.8%), in Japan (4.7%), in France (3.9%), in the USA (3.5%), and in Germany (3.0%).

The 1980s

The Greenland's GNI was $578.9 million per year in the 1980s, ranked 151st in the world, and was on a par with Laos ($580.4 million). The share in the world was 0.0038%, and 0.011% in the Americas.

The Greenland's gross national income per capita was $10 967.2 in the 1980s, ranked 31st in the world, and was on a par with Bahrain ($11.2 thousand). The GNI per capita in Greenland was greater than GNI per capita in the world ($3 117.1) in 3.5 times, and was greater than gross national income per capita in the Americas ($8 063.2) by 36.0%.

The growth of gross national income in Greenland was 3.4% in the 1980s, ranked 68th in the world, and was on a par with the Bahamas (3.4%), Portugal (3.4%). The growth of gross national income in Greenland (3.4%) was greater than growth of gross national income in the world (3.0%), was greater than growth of gross national income in the Americas (2.8%).

Comparison with neighbors. The gross national income of Greenland was less than in Canada ($372.7 billion) and in Iceland ($3.9 billion). The gross national income per capita in Greenland was less than in Iceland ($16.2 thousand) and in Canada ($14.5 thousand). The growth of GNI in Greenland was greater than in Iceland (3.0%) and in Canada (2.8%).

Comparison with leaders. The GNI of Greenland was less than in the USA ($4.2 trillion), in Japan ($1.8 trillion), in Germany ($996.5 billion), in the USSR ($887.0 billion), and in France ($732.1 billion). The Greenlandic gross national income per capita was greater than in the USSR ($3.2 thousand); but less than in the United States ($17.4 thousand), in Japan ($15.0 thousand), in France ($13.0 thousand), and in Germany ($12.8 thousand). The growth of GNI in Greenland was greater than in the USA (3.1%), in France (2.3%), and in Germany (2.0%); but less than in Japan (4.4%) and in the USSR (4.3%).

The 1990s

The Greenland's gross national income was $1.1 billion per year in the 1990s, ranked 169th in the world. The share in the world was 0.0039%, and 0.011% in the Americas.

The Greenland's GNI per capita was $20 076.3 in the 1990s, ranked 28th in the world, and was on a par with Australia ($20.2 thousand), the Bahamas ($19.9 thousand), the Virgin Islands ($19.7 thousand). The Greenlandic GNI per capita was greater than GNI per capita in the world ($4 991.4) in 4.0 times, and was greater than gross national income per capita in the Americas ($12 792.4) by 56.9%.

The growth of gross national income in Greenland was 0.3% in the 1990s, ranked 167th in the world. The growth of gross national income in Greenland (0.25%) was less than growth of gross national income in the world (2.8%), was less than growth of GNI in the Americas (3.2%).

Comparison with neighbors. The Greenland's GNI was less than in Canada ($595.6 billion) and in Iceland ($7.1 billion). The GNI per capita in Greenland was less than in Iceland ($26.6 thousand) and in Canada ($20.6 thousand). The growth of GNI in Greenland was less than in Iceland (2.5%) and in Canada (2.4%).

Comparison with leaders. The GNI of Greenland was less than in the USA ($7.5 trillion), in Japan ($4.4 trillion), in Germany ($2.2 trillion), in France ($1.4 trillion), and in the United Kingdom ($1.3 trillion). The Greenland's GNI per capita was less than in Japan ($34.7 thousand), in the United States ($28.5 thousand), in Germany ($27.0 thousand), in France ($24.3 thousand), and in the United Kingdom ($23.0 thousand). The growth of GNI in Greenland was less than in the United States (3.4%), in France (2.2%), in the UK (2.0%), in Germany (2.0%), and in Japan (1.5%).

The 2000s

The Greenlandic GNI was $1.8 billion per year in the 2000s, ranked 171st in the world. The share in the world was 0.0038%, and 0.011% in the Americas.

The Greenland's GNI per capita was $31 191.8 in the 2000s, ranked 29th in the world, and was on a par with Australasia ($32.0 thousand). The GNI per capita in Greenland was greater than GNI per capita in the world ($7 165.2) in 4.4 times, and was greater than GNI per capita in the Americas ($18 970.5) by 64.4%.

The growth of GNI in Greenland was 3.3% in the 2000s, ranked 118th in the world, and was on a par with South America (3.3%), Saint Kitts and Nevis (3.4%). The growth of GNI in Greenland (3.3%) was greater than growth of GNI in the world (3.0%), was greater than growth of gross national income in the Americas (2.1%).

Comparison with neighbors. The Greenlandic GNI was less than in Canada ($1.1 trillion) and in Iceland ($12.8 billion). The Greenlandic gross national income per capita was less than in Iceland ($43.4 thousand) and in Canada ($33.8 thousand). The growth of GNI in Greenland was greater than in Canada (2.2%) and in Iceland (1.7%).

Comparison with leaders. The Greenland's GNI was less than in the USA ($12.7 trillion), in Japan ($4.8 trillion), in Germany ($2.8 trillion), in China ($2.6 trillion), and in the United Kingdom ($2.3 trillion). The gross national income per capita in Greenland was greater than in China ($1 950.5); but less than in the USA ($43.2 thousand), in the UK ($38.5 thousand), in Japan ($37.1 thousand), and in Germany ($34.2 thousand). The growth of GNI in Greenland was greater than in the USA (1.8%), in the United Kingdom (1.7%), in Germany (1.0%), and in Japan (0.62%); but less than in China (10.4%).

The 2010s

The GNI of Greenland was $2.7 billion per year in the 2010s, ranked 175th in the world, and was on a par with Aruba ($2.7 billion). The share in the world was 0.0034%, and 0.010% in the Americas.

The Greenland's gross national income per capita was $47 245.2 in the 2010s, ranked 20th in the world, and was on a par with Canada ($47.0 thousand), Western Europe ($46.7 thousand), Finland ($48.0 thousand). The gross national income per capita in Greenland was greater than GNI per capita in the world ($10 611.7) in 4.5 times, and was greater than GNI per capita in the Americas ($26 262.7) by 79.9%.

The growth of gross national income in Greenland was 1.4% in the 2010s, ranked 166th in the world, and was on a par with Belgium (1.4%). The growth of gross national income in Greenland (1.4%) was less than growth of GNI in the world (3.1%), was less than growth of gross national income in the Americas (2.3%).

Comparison with neighbors. The Greenlandic GNI was 630.1 times lower than in Canada ($1.7 trillion) and 6.9 times lower than in Iceland ($18.5 billion). The GNI per capita in Greenland was 0.62% higher than in Canada ($47.0 thousand); but 15.9% lower than in Iceland ($56.2 thousand). The growth of GNI in Greenland was less than in Iceland (5.0%) and in Canada (2.3%).

Comparison with leaders. The GNI of Greenland was 6 858.5 times lower than in the USA ($18.3 trillion), 3 921.6 times lower than in China ($10.5 trillion), 2 022.8 times lower than in Japan ($5.4 trillion), 1 404.6 times lower than in Germany ($3.7 trillion), and 1 028.8 times lower than in France ($2.7 trillion). The gross national income per capita in Greenland was 3.2% higher than in Germany ($45.8 thousand), 11.9% higher than in Japan ($42.2 thousand), 14.1% higher than in France ($41.4 thousand), and 6.3 times higher than in China ($7.5 thousand); but 17.5% lower than in the United States ($57.3 thousand). The growth of gross national income in Greenland was greater than in Japan (1.4%) and in France (1.4%); but less than in China (7.7%), in the United States (2.5%), and in Germany (2.0%).

Part II. Structure

	The 2010s
agriculture	17.4%
industry	8.4%
construction	9.8%
trade	10.4%
transportation	12.3%
services	41.7%

Chapter IV. Agriculture

Agriculture, hunting, forestry, fishing (ISIC A-B)

The value added of agriculture in Greenland grew from $39.3 million per year in the 1970s to $461.9 million per year in the 2010s, that is by $422.6 million or 11.8 times. The change occurred at $376.4 million due to a 5.4-fold increase in prices, as also at $40.1 million due to a 1.9-fold increase in productivity, as well as at $6.2 million due to the rise in population. The average annual growth in agriculture is 2.4%. The minimum value of agriculture was in 1970 at $13.1 million. The maximum value of agriculture was in 2019 at $559.7 million.

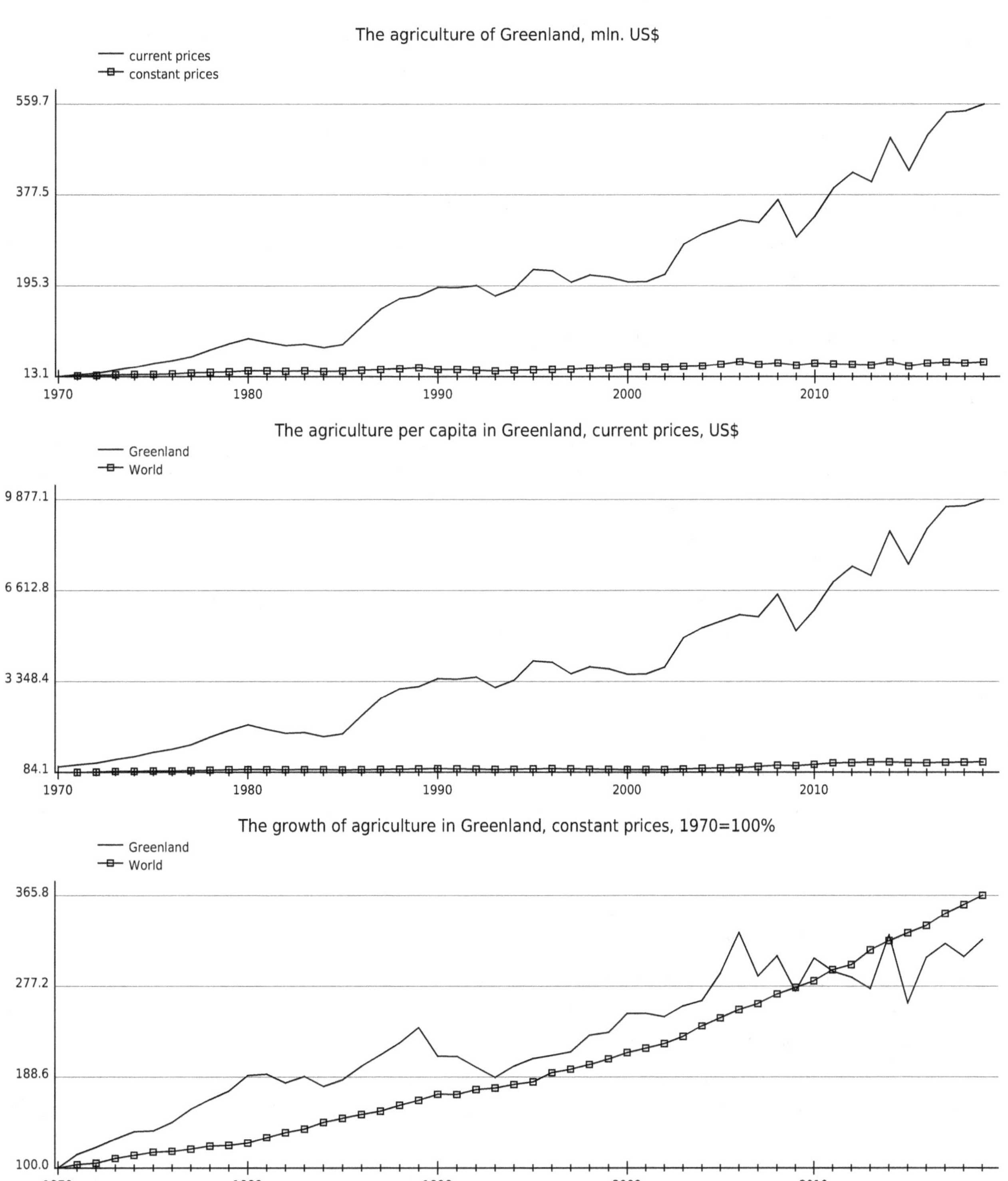

The share of agriculture in the economy of Greenland, %

The 1970s

The agriculture of Greenland was $39.3 million per year in the 1970s, ranked 136th in the world, and was on a par with French Polynesia ($39.1 million). The share in the world was 0.0076%, and 0.044% in the Americas.

The share of agriculture in the economy of Greenland was 17.5% in the 1970s, ranked 80th in the world.

The Greenlandic agriculture per capita was $804.8 in the 1970s, ranked 1st in the world. The Greenlandic agriculture per capita was greater than agriculture per capita in the world ($127.6) in 6.3 times, and was greater than agriculture per capita in the Americas ($158.1) in 5.1 times.

The growth of agriculture in Greenland was 6.4% in the 1970s, ranked 28th in the world, and was on a par with Eastern Europe (6.4%). The growth of agriculture in Greenland (6.4%) was greater than growth of agriculture in the world (2.2%), was greater than growth of agriculture in the Americas (1.9%).

Comparison with neighbors. The Greenlandic agriculture was less than in Canada ($6.9 billion) and in Iceland ($154.0 million). The agriculture per capita in Greenland was greater than in Iceland ($712.7) and in Canada ($303.2). The growth of agriculture in Greenland was greater than in Iceland (5.3%) and in Canada (0.17%).

Comparison with leaders. The sector of agriculture in Greenland was less than in the USSR ($88.7 billion), in China ($49.5 billion), in the United States ($42.6 billion), in India ($36.0 billion), and in Japan ($25.8 billion). The agriculture per capita in Greenland was greater than in the USSR ($351.8), in Japan ($231.3), in the United States ($195.0), in India ($58.3), and in China ($54.2). The growth of agriculture in Greenland was greater than in China (2.4%), in Japan (0.52%), in the USA (0.34%), and in India (0.30%); but less than in the USSR (7.0%).

The 1980s

The value added of agriculture in Greenland was $108.2 million per year in the 1980s, ranked 134th in the world. The share in the world was 0.012%, and 0.069% in the Americas.

The share of agriculture in the economy of Greenland was 17.5% in the 1980s, ranked 73rd in the world, and was on a par with Morocco (17.5%), Tuvalu (17.6%).

The value added of agriculture per capita in Greenland was $2 050.2 in the 1980s, ranked 1st in the world. The sector of agriculture per capita in Greenland was greater than agriculture per capita in the world ($186.6) in 11.0 times, and was greater than agriculture per capita in the Americas ($237.6) in 8.6 times.

The growth of agriculture in Greenland was 3.1% in the 1980s, ranked 66th in the world, and was on a par with Northern Africa (3.1%), Ireland (3.1%), Cameroon (3.1%). The growth of agriculture in Greenland (3.1%) was less than growth of agriculture in the world (3.1%), was greater than growth of agriculture in the Americas (2.6%).

Comparison with neighbors. The Greenland's agriculture was less than in Canada ($12.4 billion) and in Iceland ($374.6 million). The agriculture per capita in Greenland was greater than in Iceland ($1 559.3) and in Canada ($482.3). The growth of agriculture in Greenland was greater than in Iceland (2.6%) and in Canada (2.5%).

Comparison with leaders. The value added of agriculture in Greenland was less than in the USSR ($125.8 billion), in China ($94.9

billion), in India ($70.4 billion), in the USA ($68.7 billion), and in Japan ($49.7 billion). The value of agriculture per capita in Greenland was greater than in the USSR ($457.2), in Japan ($410.0), in the USA ($286.8), in India ($90.7), and in China ($88.5). The growth of agriculture in Greenland was greater than in the USSR (2.8%) and in Japan (0.41%); but less than in China (5.3%), in India (4.4%), and in the United States (3.7%).

The 1990s

The value of agriculture in Greenland was $202.9 million per year in the 1990s, ranked 152nd in the world. The share in the world was 0.018%, and 0.091% in the Americas.

The share of agriculture in the economy of Greenland was 17.5% in the 1990s, ranked 80th in the world, and was on a par with Morocco (17.6%), the Philippines (17.6%), Micronesia (17.3%).

The value of agriculture per capita in Greenland was $3 632.6 in the 1990s, ranked 1st in the world. The value added of agriculture per capita in Greenland was greater than agriculture per capita in the world ($199.8) in 18.2 times, and was greater than agriculture per capita in the Americas ($288.9) in 12.6 times.

The growth of agriculture in Greenland was -0.2% in the 1990s, ranked 148th in the world. The growth of agriculture in Greenland (-0.20%) was less than growth of agriculture in the world (2.2%), was less than growth of agriculture in the Americas (2.4%).

Comparison with neighbors. The sector of agriculture in Greenland was less than in Canada ($15.3 billion) and in Iceland ($648.8 million). The agriculture per capita in Greenland was greater than in Iceland ($2.4 thousand) and in Canada ($527.4). The growth of agriculture in Greenland was greater than in Iceland (-1.2%); but less than in Canada (1.1%).

Comparison with leaders. The value of agriculture in Greenland was less than in China ($139.0 billion), in the United States ($96.1 billion), in India ($91.4 billion), in Japan ($78.9 billion), and in Brazil ($36.8 billion). The sector of agriculture per capita in Greenland was greater than in Japan ($625.5), in the United States ($363.4), in Brazil ($228.7), in China ($112.7), and in India ($95.6). The growth of agriculture in Greenland was greater than in Japan (-1.8%); but less than in China (4.3%), in Brazil (3.0%), in India (2.8%), and in the USA (2.6%).

The 2000s

The value of agriculture in Greenland was $282.7 million per year in the 2000s, ranked 150th in the world, and was on a par with Swaziland ($287.0 million). The share in the world was 0.018%, and 0.098% in the Americas.

The share of agriculture in the economy of Greenland was 16.1% in the 2000s, ranked 63rd in the world, and was on a par with Micronesia (16.0%).

The Greenlandic agriculture per capita was $4 986.1 in the 2000s, ranked 1st in the world. The value added of agriculture per capita in Greenland was greater than agriculture per capita in the world ($240.3) in 20.7 times, and was greater than agriculture per capita in the Americas ($327.5) in 15.2 times.

The growth of agriculture in Greenland was 1.6% in the 2000s, ranked 121st in the world, and was on a par with Papua New Guinea (1.6%). The growth of agriculture in Greenland (1.6%) was less than growth of agriculture in the world (3.0%), was less than growth of agriculture in the Americas (2.7%).

Comparison with neighbors. The value added of agriculture in Greenland was less than in Canada ($20.3 billion) and in Iceland ($754.7 million). The agriculture per capita in Greenland was greater than in Iceland ($2.6 thousand) and in Canada ($634.5). The growth of agriculture in Greenland was greater than in Canada (1.2%) and in Iceland (-0.0075%).

Comparison with leaders. The Greenlandic agriculture was less than in China ($297.7 billion), in India ($147.6 billion), in the USA ($122.5 billion), in Japan ($57.1 billion), and in Nigeria ($47.6 billion). The agriculture per capita in Greenland was greater than in Japan ($445.6), in the USA ($416.9), in Nigeria ($346.4), in China ($224.5), and in India ($129.7). The growth of agriculture in Greenland was greater than in Japan (-1.3%); but less than in Nigeria (10.1%), in China (4.0%), in the United States (3.6%), and in India (2.0%).

The 2010s

The value added of agriculture in Greenland was $461.9 million per year in the 2010s, ranked 148th in the world. The share in the world was 0.015%, and 0.095% in the Americas.

The share of agriculture in the economy of Greenland was 17.4% in the 2010s, ranked 55th in the world, and was on a par with Eritrea (17.4%), Micronesia (17.3%).

The value added of agriculture per capita in Greenland was $8 176.1 in the 2010s, ranked 1st in the world. The Greenlandic agriculture per capita was greater than agriculture per capita in the world ($432.1) in 18.9 times, and was greater than agriculture per capita in the Americas ($498.8) in 16.4 times.

The growth of agriculture in Greenland was 1.7% in the 2010s, ranked 114th in the world. The growth of agriculture in Greenland (1.7%) was less than growth of agriculture in the world (2.9%), was less than growth of agriculture in the Americas (2.2%).

Comparison with neighbors. The value of agriculture in Greenland was 65.5 times lower than in Canada ($30.3 billion) and 2.1 times lower than in Iceland ($947.0 million). The value added of agriculture per capita in Greenland was 2.8 times higher than in Iceland ($2.9 thousand) and 9.7 times higher than in Canada ($845.0). The growth of agriculture in Greenland was greater than in Iceland (1.5%); but less than in Canada (3.4%).

Comparison with leaders. The value added of agriculture in Greenland was 1 918.6 times lower than in China ($886.2 billion), 786.7 times lower than in India ($363.4 billion), 390.3 times lower than in the USA ($180.3 billion), 268.6 times lower than in Indonesia ($124.1 billion), and 207.3 times lower than in Nigeria ($95.8 billion). The sector of agriculture per capita in Greenland was 12.9 times higher than in China ($631.9), 14.5 times higher than in the USA ($564.3), 15.3 times higher than in Nigeria ($534.6), 16.9 times higher than in Indonesia ($483.6), and 29.3 times higher than in India ($279.1). The growth of agriculture in Greenland was less than in India (4.1%), in Indonesia (3.9%), in China (3.8%), in Nigeria (3.6%), and in the United States (2.0%).

Chapter V. Industry

Mining, Manufacturing, Utilities (ISIC C-E)

The industry of Greenland enlarged from $23.5 million per year in the 1970s to $221.9 million per year in the 2010s, that is by $198.4 million or 9.5 times. The change occurred at $169.3 million due to a 4.2-fold increase in prices, as also at $25.4 million due to a 1.9-fold increase in productivity, as well as at $3.7 million due to the increase in population. The average annual growth in industry is 2.7%. The minimum value of industry was in 1970 at $7.8 million. The maximum value of industry was in 2012 at $255.8 million.

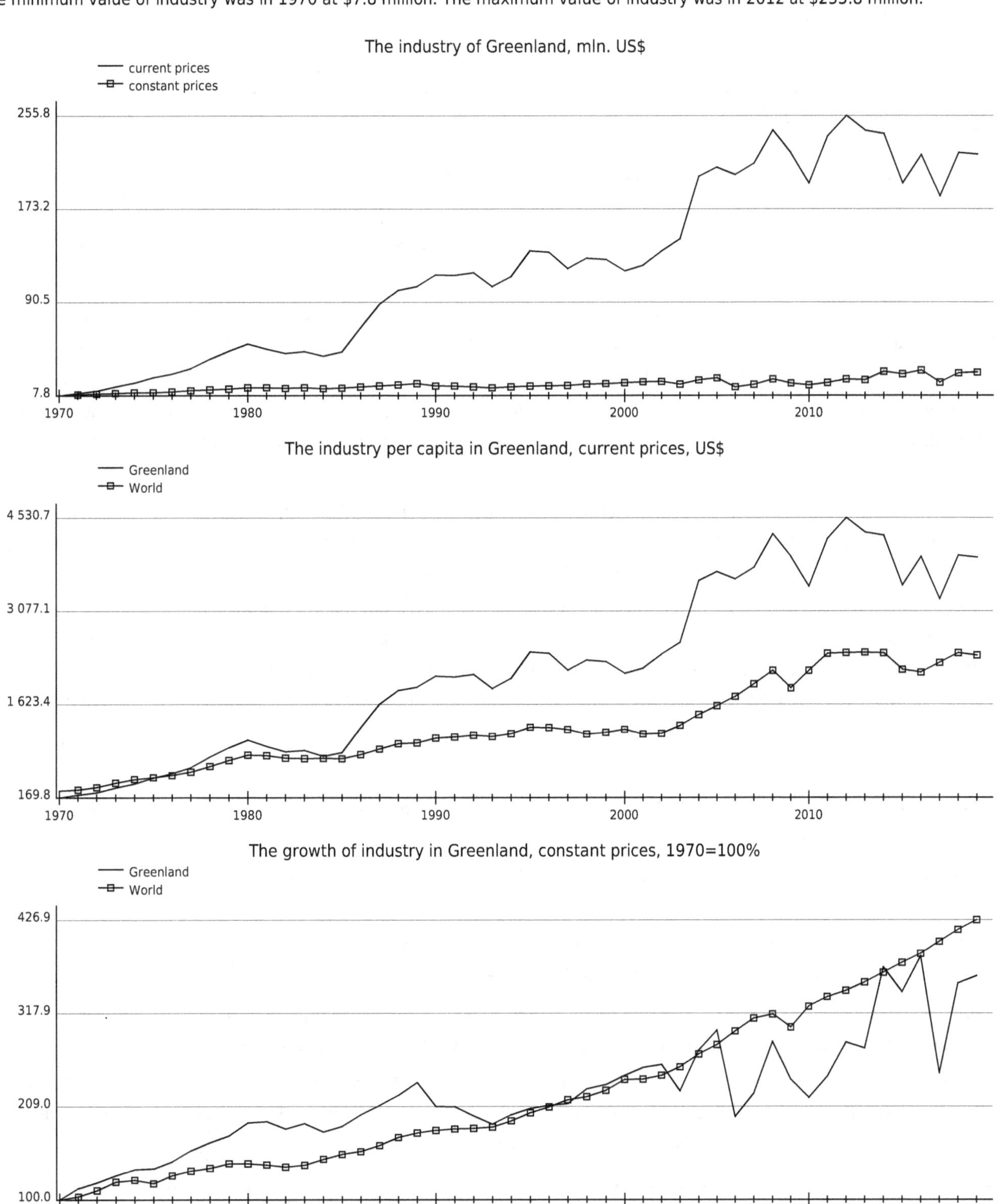

The industry of Greenland, mln. US$

The industry per capita in Greenland, current prices, US$

The growth of industry in Greenland, constant prices, 1970=100%

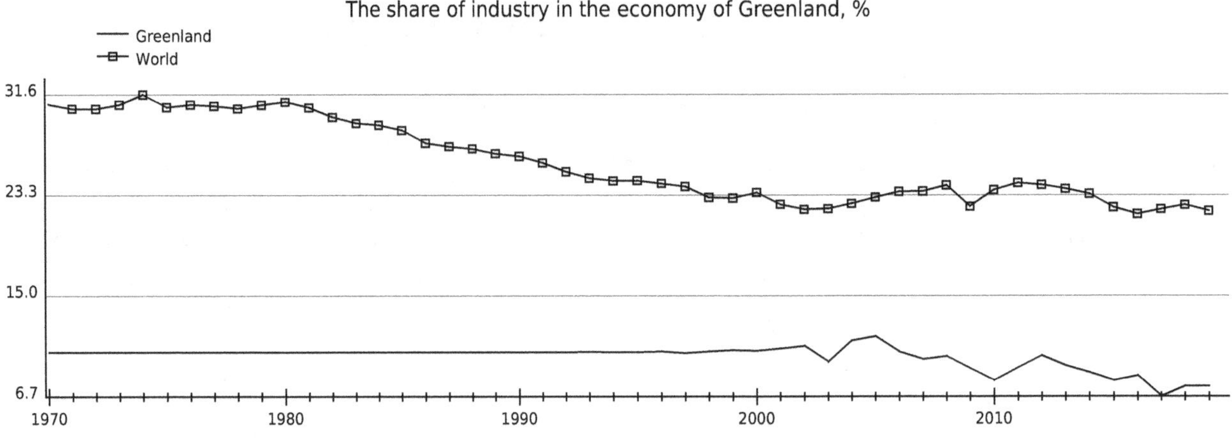

The 1970s

The industry of Greenland was $23.5 million per year in the 1970s, ranked 150th in the world. The share in the world was 0.0012%, and 0.0038% in the Americas.

The share of industry in the economy of Greenland was 10.4% in the 1970s, ranked 147th in the world, and was on a par with Sudan (10.5%).

The sector of industry per capita in Greenland was $480.5 in the 1970s, ranked 52nd in the world, and was on a par with the World ($480.5), Andorra ($477.6), South Africa ($469.8). The value added of industry per capita in Greenland was greater than industry per capita in the world ($480.5) by 0.017%, and was less than industry per capita in the Americas ($1 091.1) in 2.3 times.

The growth of industry in Greenland was 6.4% in the 1970s, ranked 62nd in the world, and was on a par with Malawi (6.4%). The growth of industry in Greenland (6.4%) was greater than growth of industry in the world (4.0%), was greater than growth of industry in the Americas (3.2%).

Comparison with neighbors. The industry of Greenland was less than in Canada ($44.9 billion) and in Iceland ($298.7 million). The sector of industry per capita in Greenland was less than in Canada ($1 963.4) and in Iceland ($1 382.4). The growth of industry in Greenland was greater than in Canada (3.2%); but less than in Iceland (6.8%).

Comparison with leaders. The sector of industry in Greenland was less than in the USA ($450.4 billion), in the USSR ($248.8 billion), in Japan ($185.6 billion), in Germany ($158.4 billion), and in the United Kingdom ($72.6 billion). The Greenlandic industry per capita was less than in the USA ($2.1 thousand), in Germany ($2.0 thousand), in Japan ($1 666.5), in the United Kingdom ($1 295.1), and in the USSR ($986.6). The growth of industry in Greenland was greater than in the USSR (5.2%), in Japan (4.5%), in the United States (2.4%), in Germany (2.1%), and in the UK (1.9%).

The 1980s

The value added of industry in Greenland was $64.6 million per year in the 1980s, ranked 148th in the world. The share in the world was 0.0016%, and 0.0047% in the Americas.

The share of industry in the economy of Greenland was 10.4% in the 1980s, ranked 146th in the world.

The industry per capita in Greenland was $1 224.2 in the 1980s, ranked 42nd in the world, and was on a par with Western Asia ($1 249.8). The value added of industry per capita in Greenland was greater than industry per capita in the world ($861.8) by 42.0%, and was less than industry per capita in the Americas ($2 085.6) by 41.3%.

The growth of industry in Greenland was 3.1% in the 1980s, ranked 89th in the world. The growth of industry in Greenland (3.1%) was greater than growth of industry in the world (2.3%), was greater than growth of industry in the Americas (1.9%).

Comparison with neighbors. The value of industry in Greenland was less than in Canada ($99.2 billion) and in Iceland ($839.9 million). The sector of industry per capita in Greenland was less than in Canada ($3.9 thousand) and in Iceland ($3.5 thousand). The growth of industry in Greenland was greater than in Iceland (1.9%) and in Canada (1.9%).

Comparison with leaders. The sector of industry in Greenland was less than in the United States ($1.0 trillion), in Japan ($566.4 billion), in the USSR ($305.7 billion), in Germany ($297.5 billion), and in the UK ($171.2 billion). The value of industry per capita in

Greenland was greater than in the USSR ($1 110.8); but less than in Japan ($4.7 thousand), in the United States ($4.2 thousand), in Germany ($3.8 thousand), and in the UK ($3.0 thousand). The growth of industry in Greenland was greater than in the United States (1.9%), in the United Kingdom (1.4%), and in Germany (1.2%); but less than in the USSR (5.3%) and in Japan (4.2%).

The 1990s

The value added of industry in Greenland was $121.3 million per year in the 1990s, ranked 168th in the world, and was on a par with Bermuda ($121.1 million). The share in the world was 0.0018%, and 0.0058% in the Americas.

The share of industry in the economy of Greenland was 10.4% in the 1990s, ranked 168th in the world, and was on a par with Nepal (10.4%).

The value of industry per capita in Greenland was $2 171.2 in the 1990s, ranked 40th in the world, and was on a par with Hong Kong ($2.1 thousand). The Greenland's industry per capita was greater than industry per capita in the world ($1 175.6) by 84.7%, and was less than industry per capita in the Americas ($2 704.1) by 19.7%.

The growth of industry in Greenland was -0.1% in the 1990s, ranked 157th in the world. The growth of industry in Greenland (-0.095%) was less than growth of industry in the world (2.5%), was less than growth of industry in the Americas (2.8%).

Comparison with neighbors. The sector of industry in Greenland was less than in Canada ($138.6 billion) and in Iceland ($1.3 billion). The sector of industry per capita in Greenland was less than in Iceland ($4.8 thousand) and in Canada ($4.8 thousand). The growth of industry in Greenland was less than in Canada (2.5%) and in Iceland (1.7%).

Comparison with leaders. The Greenland's industry was less than in the USA ($1.5 trillion), in Japan ($1.2 trillion), in Germany ($534.0 billion), in China ($285.9 billion), and in the UK ($268.6 billion). The industry per capita in Greenland was greater than in China ($231.9); but less than in Japan ($9.4 thousand), in Germany ($6.6 thousand), in the USA ($5.7 thousand), and in the United Kingdom ($4.6 thousand). The growth of industry in Greenland was less than in China (13.1%), in the United States (2.8%), in Japan (1.3%), in the UK (1.2%), and in Germany (0.33%).

The 2000s

The Greenlandic industry was $181.9 million per year in the 2000s, ranked 170th in the world. The share in the world was 0.0018%, and 0.0059% in the Americas.

The share of industry in the economy of Greenland was 10.3% in the 2000s, ranked 169th in the world, and was on a par with Nepal (10.3%), Albania (10.4%), Cabo Verde (10.4%).

The value of industry per capita in Greenland was $3 208.3 in the 2000s, ranked 43rd in the world. The sector of industry per capita in Greenland was greater than industry per capita in the world ($1 573.8) in 2.0 times, and was less than industry per capita in the Americas ($3 499.5) by 8.3%.

The growth of industry in Greenland was 0.2% in the 2000s, ranked 166th in the world. The growth of industry in Greenland (0.24%) was less than growth of industry in the world (2.9%), was less than growth of industry in the Americas (1.4%).

Comparison with neighbors. The industry of Greenland was less than in Canada ($246.3 billion) and in Iceland ($1.9 billion). The industry per capita in Greenland was less than in Canada ($7.7 thousand) and in Iceland ($6.5 thousand). The growth of industry in Greenland was greater than in Canada (-0.63%); but less than in Iceland (2.7%).

Comparison with leaders. The Greenland's industry was less than in the United States ($2.1 trillion), in Japan ($1.1 trillion), in China ($1.1 trillion), in Germany ($629.4 billion), and in the United Kingdom ($345.1 billion). The value added of industry per capita in Greenland was greater than in China ($795.3); but less than in Japan ($8.8 thousand), in Germany ($7.7 thousand), in the USA ($7.1 thousand), and in the UK ($5.7 thousand). The growth of industry in Greenland was greater than in Germany (0.19%), in Japan (0.15%), and in the UK (-1.1%); but less than in China (11.1%) and in the USA (1.5%).

The 2010s

The industry of Greenland was $221.9 million per year in the 2010s, ranked 173rd in the world, and was on a par with Aruba ($221.0 million). The share in the world was 0.0013%, and 0.0052% in the Americas.

The share of industry in the economy of Greenland was 8.4% in the 2010s, ranked 176th in the world.

The value added of industry per capita in Greenland was $3 927.8 in the 2010s, ranked 45th in the world, and was on a par with Gabon

($4.0 thousand). The value added of industry per capita in Greenland was greater than industry per capita in the world ($2 320.9) by 69.2%, and was less than industry per capita in the Americas ($4 354.8) by 9.8%.

The growth of industry in Greenland was 4.2% in the 2010s, ranked 65th in the world, and was on a par with Lithuania (4.2%), Zambia (4.2%). The growth of industry in Greenland (4.2%) was greater than growth of industry in the world (3.5%), was greater than growth of industry in the Americas (1.8%).

Comparison with neighbors. The Greenland's industry was 1 384.8 times lower than in Canada ($307.3 billion) and 12.8 times lower than in Iceland ($2.8 billion). The sector of industry per capita in Greenland was 2.2 times lower than in Iceland ($8.6 thousand) and 2.2 times lower than in Canada ($8.6 thousand). The growth of industry in Greenland was greater than in Iceland (2.5%) and in Canada (2.5%).

Comparison with leaders. The Greenland's industry was 16 597.7 times lower than in China ($3.7 trillion), 12 354.8 times lower than in the USA ($2.7 trillion), 5 364.4 times lower than in Japan ($1.2 trillion), 3 785.2 times lower than in Germany ($840.0 billion), and 1 998.0 times lower than in India ($443.4 billion). The sector of industry per capita in Greenland was 49.6% higher than in China ($2.6 thousand) and 11.5 times higher than in India ($340.6); but 2.6 times lower than in Germany ($10.3 thousand), 2.4 times lower than in Japan ($9.3 thousand), and 2.2 times lower than in the USA ($8.6 thousand). The growth of industry in Greenland was greater than in Germany (3.2%), in Japan (2.6%), and in the United States (2.2%); but less than in China (7.5%) and in India (6.5%).

Chapter 5.1. Manufacturing

(ISIC D)

The Greenlandic manufacturing grew from $16.6 million per year in the 1970s to $121.0 million per year in the 2010s, that is by $104.4 million or 7.3 times. The change occurred at $93.4 million due to a 4.4-fold increase in prices, as also at $8.5 million due to a 1.4-fold increase in productivity, as well as at $2.6 million due to the growing in population. The average annual growth in manufacturing is 1.9%. The minimum value of manufacturing was in 1970 at $5.5 million. The maximum value of manufacturing was in 2005 at $153.8 million.

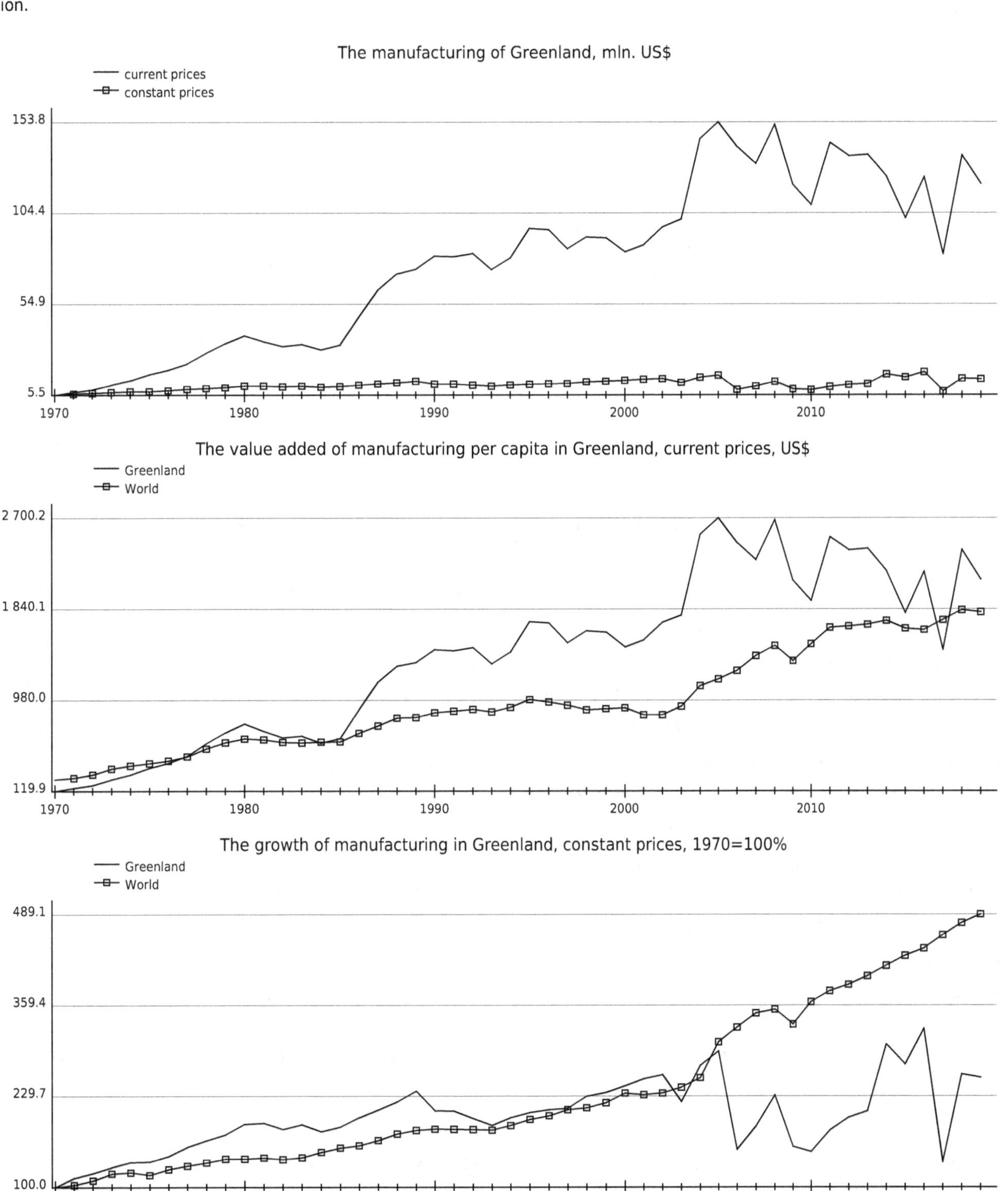

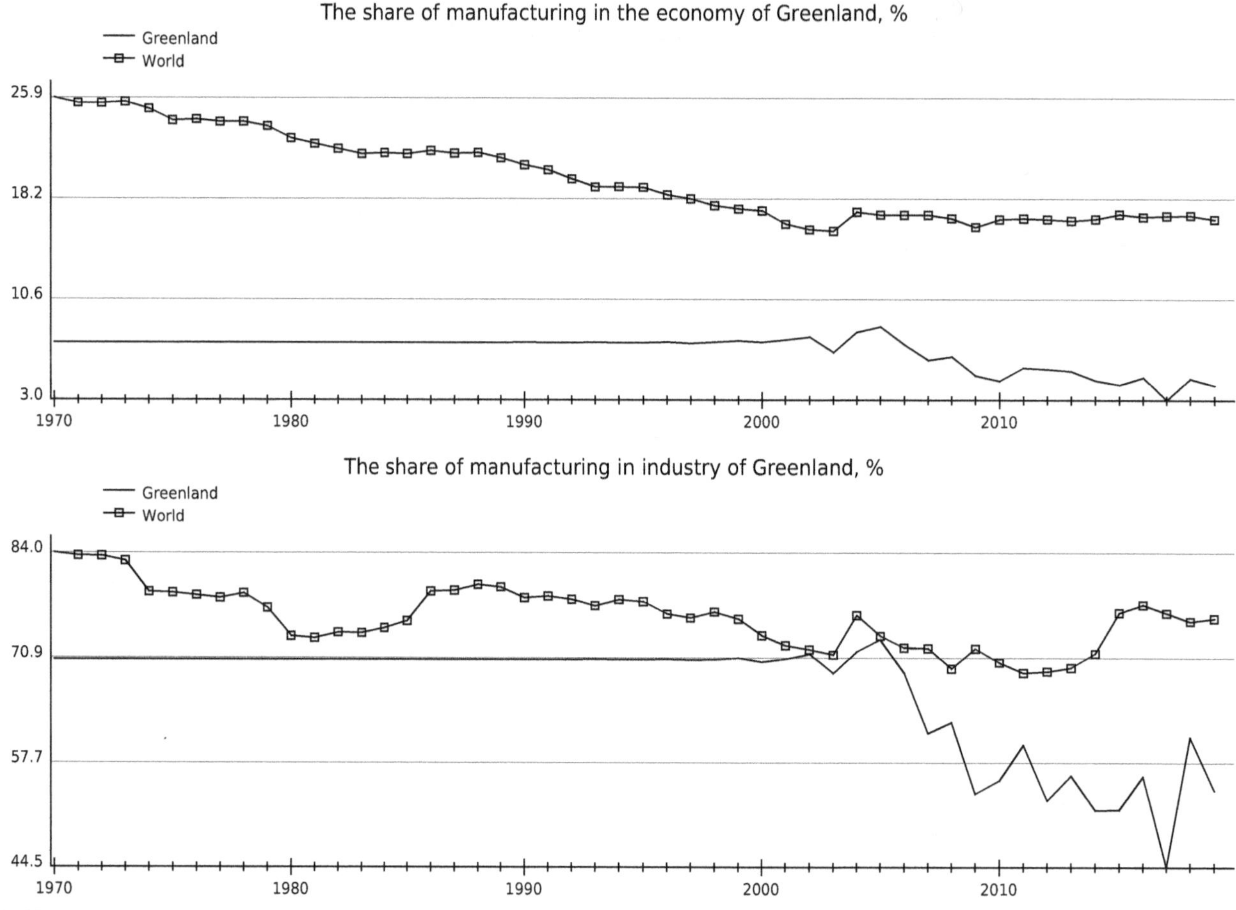

The 1970s

The manufacturing of Greenland was $16.6 million per year in the 1970s, ranked 147th in the world. The share in the world was 0.0011%, and 0.0033% in the Americas.

The share of manufacturing in the economy of Greenland was 7.4% in the 1970s, ranked 135th in the world, and was on a par with Polynesia (7.4%), Rwanda (7.3%), Botswana (7.4%).

The manufacturing per capita in Greenland was $339.5 in the 1970s, ranked 45th in the world, and was on a par with Mexico ($335.7). The Greenlandic manufacturing per capita was less than manufacturing per capita in the world ($383.2) by 11.4%, and was less than manufacturing per capita in the Americas ($896.7) in 2.6 times.

The growth of manufacturing in Greenland was 6.4% in the 1970s, ranked 59th in the world, and was on a par with Saint Lucia (6.4%), Italy (6.4%). The growth of manufacturing in Greenland (6.4%) was greater than growth of manufacturing in the world (3.8%), was greater than growth of manufacturing in the Americas (3.6%).

Comparison with neighbors. The Greenland's manufacturing was less than in Canada ($31.6 billion) and in Iceland ($249.8 million). The sector of manufacturing per capita in Greenland was less than in Canada ($1 382.9) and in Iceland ($1 156.0). The growth of manufacturing in Greenland was greater than in Canada (4.5%); but less than in Iceland (6.7%).

Comparison with leaders. The value added of manufacturing in Greenland was less than in the USA ($378.0 billion), in the USSR ($248.8 billion), in Japan ($169.3 billion), in Germany ($138.0 billion), and in France ($64.5 billion). The value added of manufacturing per capita in Greenland was less than in Germany ($1 752.1), in the USA ($1 731.8), in Japan ($1 520.6), in France ($1 203.0), and in the USSR ($986.6). The growth of manufacturing in Greenland was greater than in the USSR (5.2%), in Japan (4.5%), in France (3.5%), in the USA (2.7%), and in Germany (2.1%).

The 1980s

The Greenlandic manufacturing was $45.6 million per year in the 1980s, ranked 146th in the world. The share in the world was 0.0014%, and 0.0043% in the Americas.

The share of manufacturing in the economy of Greenland was 7.4% in the 1980s, ranked 139th in the world, and was on a par with Sudan (7.3%).

The manufacturing per capita in Greenland was $864.8 in the 1980s, ranked 41st in the world, and was on a par with French Polynesia ($857.8). The value added of manufacturing per capita in Greenland was greater than manufacturing per capita in the world ($661.2) by 30.8%, and was less than manufacturing per capita in the Americas ($1 597.5) by 45.9%.

The growth of manufacturing in Greenland was 3.1% in the 1980s, ranked 91st in the world, and was on a par with Malawi (3.1%), Chile (3.1%). The growth of manufacturing in Greenland (3.1%) was greater than growth of manufacturing in the world (2.6%), was greater than growth of manufacturing in the Americas (1.8%).

Comparison with neighbors. The value of manufacturing in Greenland was less than in Canada ($64.9 billion) and in Iceland ($659.0 million). The manufacturing per capita in Greenland was less than in Iceland ($2.7 thousand) and in Canada ($2.5 thousand). The growth of manufacturing in Greenland was greater than in Canada (2.2%) and in Iceland (1.1%).

Comparison with leaders. The sector of manufacturing in Greenland was less than in the USA ($789.4 billion), in Japan ($501.0 billion), in the USSR ($305.7 billion), in Germany ($258.7 billion), and in Italy ($134.1 billion). The value of manufacturing per capita in Greenland was less than in Japan ($4.1 thousand), in Germany ($3.3 thousand), in the United States ($3.3 thousand), in Italy ($2.4 thousand), and in the USSR ($1 110.8). The growth of manufacturing in Greenland was greater than in Italy (2.5%), in the USA (1.9%), and in Germany (1.2%); but less than in the USSR (5.3%) and in Japan (4.4%).

The 1990s

The Greenlandic manufacturing was $85.7 million per year in the 1990s, ranked 166th in the world. The share in the world was 0.0017%, and 0.0051% in the Americas.

The share of manufacturing in the economy of Greenland was 7.4% in the 1990s, ranked 160th in the world, and was on a par with Guinea-Bissau (7.3%), Saint Kitts and Nevis (7.4%).

The value of manufacturing per capita in Greenland was $1 534.1 in the 1990s, ranked 37th in the world. The Greenlandic manufacturing per capita was greater than manufacturing per capita in the world ($908.4) by 68.9%, and was less than manufacturing per capita in the Americas ($2 172.9) by 29.4%.

The growth of manufacturing in Greenland was -0.1% in the 1990s, ranked 152nd in the world. The growth of manufacturing in Greenland (-0.073%) was less than growth of manufacturing in the world (2.0%), was less than growth of manufacturing in the Americas (3.0%).

Comparison with neighbors. The value of manufacturing in Greenland was less than in Canada ($97.8 billion) and in Iceland ($1.0 billion). The value of manufacturing per capita in Greenland was less than in Iceland ($3.8 thousand) and in Canada ($3.4 thousand). The growth of manufacturing in Greenland was less than in Canada (2.7%) and in Iceland (1.4%).

Comparison with leaders. The manufacturing of Greenland was less than in the USA ($1.2 trillion), in Japan ($1.0 trillion), in Germany ($468.8 billion), in Italy ($227.8 billion), and in France ($215.0 billion). The sector of manufacturing per capita in Greenland was less than in Japan ($8.3 thousand), in Germany ($5.8 thousand), in the United States ($4.7 thousand), in Italy ($4.0 thousand), and in France ($3.6 thousand). The growth of manufacturing in Greenland was less than in the USA (3.2%), in France (2.4%), in Italy (1.2%), in Japan (1.1%), and in Germany (0.26%).

The 2000s

The value of manufacturing in Greenland was $121.0 million per year in the 2000s, ranked 168th in the world. The share in the world was 0.0016%, and 0.0053% in the Americas.

The share of manufacturing in the economy of Greenland was 6.9% in the 2000s, ranked 158th in the world, and was on a par with São Tomé and Príncipe (6.9%), Saint Kitts and Nevis (6.9%), Congo (6.9%).

The manufacturing per capita in Greenland was $2 134.9 in the 2000s, ranked 38th in the world, and was on a par with Malta ($2.1 thousand). The value of manufacturing per capita in Greenland was greater than manufacturing per capita in the world ($1 138.1) by 87.6%, and was less than manufacturing per capita in the Americas ($2 583.7) by 17.4%.

The growth of manufacturing in Greenland was -3.9% in the 2000s, ranked 199th in the world. The growth of manufacturing in

Greenland (-3.9%) was less than growth of manufacturing in the world (4.2%), was less than growth of manufacturing in the Americas (1.4%).

Comparison with neighbors. The Greenland's manufacturing was less than in Canada ($144.4 billion) and in Iceland ($1.4 billion). The value added of manufacturing per capita in Greenland was less than in Iceland ($4.7 thousand) and in Canada ($4.5 thousand). The growth of manufacturing in Greenland was less than in Iceland (1.4%) and in Canada (-1.5%).

Comparison with leaders. The value of manufacturing in Greenland was less than in the United States ($1.6 trillion), in China ($1.1 trillion), in Japan ($992.9 billion), in Germany ($551.4 billion), and in Italy ($277.2 billion). The value of manufacturing per capita in Greenland was greater than in China ($815.3); but less than in Japan ($7.7 thousand), in Germany ($6.8 thousand), in the United States ($5.6 thousand), and in Italy ($4.8 thousand). The growth of manufacturing in Greenland was less than in the USA (1.6%), in Japan (0.32%), in Germany (0.097%), and in Italy (-1.3%).

The 2010s

The value added of manufacturing in Greenland was $121.0 million per year in the 2010s, ranked 174th in the world, and was on a par with Eritrea ($123.7 million). The share in the world was 0.0010%, and 0.0040% in the Americas.

The share of manufacturing in the economy of Greenland was 4.6% in the 2010s, ranked 178th in the world.

The sector of manufacturing per capita in Greenland was $2 141.9 in the 2010s, ranked 51st in the world. The value added of manufacturing per capita in Greenland was greater than manufacturing per capita in the world ($1 697.4) by 26.2%, and was less than manufacturing per capita in the Americas ($3 100.6) by 30.9%.

The growth of manufacturing in Greenland was 5% in the 2010s, ranked 49th in the world, and was on a par with Macedonia (4.9%), South-Eastern Asia (4.9%). The growth of manufacturing in Greenland (5.0%) was greater than growth of manufacturing in the world (3.9%), was greater than growth of manufacturing in the Americas (1.6%).

Comparison with neighbors. The value added of manufacturing in Greenland was 1 389.5 times lower than in Canada ($168.1 billion) and 16.1 times lower than in Iceland ($1.9 billion). The value added of manufacturing per capita in Greenland was 2.8 times lower than in Iceland ($5.9 thousand) and 2.2 times lower than in Canada ($4.7 thousand). The growth of manufacturing in Greenland was greater than in Iceland (3.1%) and in Canada (1.7%).

Comparison with leaders. The value added of manufacturing in Greenland was 25 742.7 times lower than in China ($3.1 trillion), 17 110.5 times lower than in the United States ($2.1 trillion), 8 759.7 times lower than in Japan ($1.1 trillion), 6 075.5 times lower than in Germany ($735.2 billion), and 3 227.1 times lower than in South Korea ($390.5 billion). The value of manufacturing per capita in Greenland was 4.2 times lower than in Germany ($9.0 thousand), 3.9 times lower than in Japan ($8.3 thousand), 3.6 times lower than in South Korea ($7.7 thousand), 3.0 times lower than in the United States ($6.5 thousand), and 3.6% lower than in China ($2.2 thousand). The growth of manufacturing in Greenland was greater than in Republic of Korea (3.8%), in Germany (3.5%), in Japan (3.0%), and in the USA (1.9%); but less than in China (7.5%).

Chapter VI. Construction

(ISIC F)

The value of construction in Greenland rose from $11.3 million per year in the 1970s to $259.9 million per year in the 2010s, that is by $248.6 million or 23.0 times. The change occurred at $199.8 million due to a 4.3-fold increase in prices, as also at $47.0 million due to a 4.6-fold increase in productivity, as well as at $1.8 million due to the expansion in population. The average annual growth in construction is 4.7%. The minimum value of construction was in 1970 at $3.8 million. The maximum value of construction was in 2018 at $315.3 million.

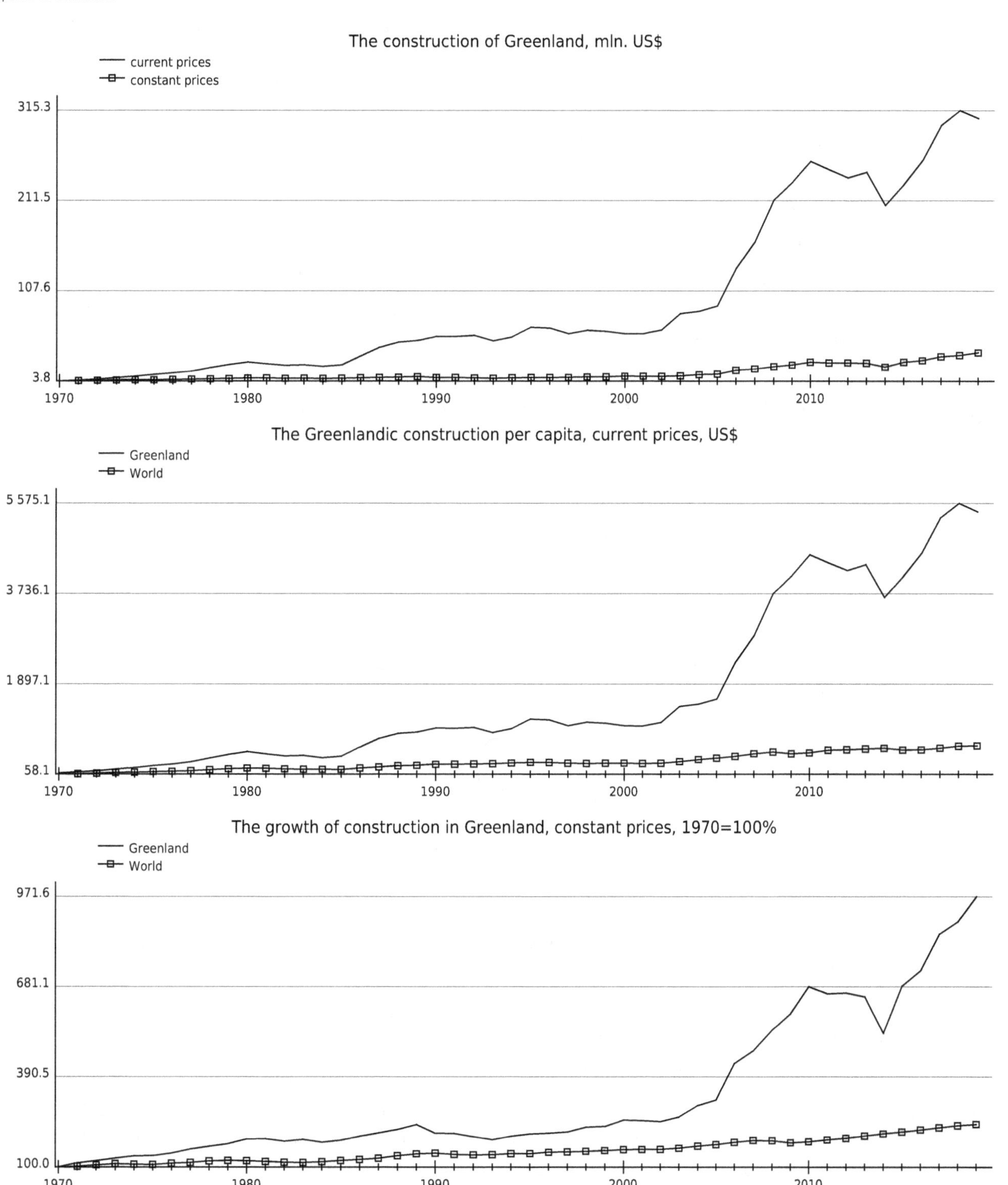

The construction of Greenland, mln. US$

The Greenlandic construction per capita, current prices, US$

The growth of construction in Greenland, constant prices, 1970=100%

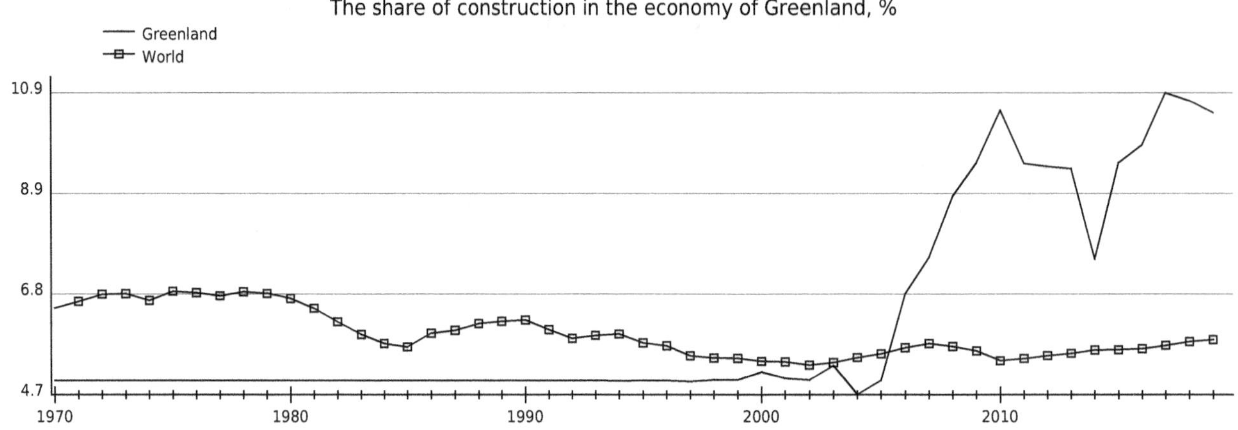

The 1970s

The value added of construction in Greenland was $11.3 million per year in the 1970s, ranked 150th in the world, and was on a par with Bhutan ($11.1 million). The share in the world was 0.0026%, and 0.0093% in the Americas.

The share of construction in the economy of Greenland was 5.0% in the 1970s, ranked 118th in the world, and was on a par with Northern America (5.0%), Belize (5.0%), Haiti (5.1%).

The value added of construction per capita in Greenland was $231.9 in the 1970s, ranked 44th in the world. The sector of construction per capita in Greenland was greater than construction per capita in the world ($106.1) in 2.2 times, and was greater than construction per capita in the Americas ($217.5) by 6.6%.

The growth of construction in Greenland was 6.4% in the 1970s, ranked 69th in the world, and was on a par with Liberia (6.3%), Hungary (6.4%), Pakistan (6.4%). The growth of construction in Greenland (6.4%) was greater than growth of construction in the world (2.1%), was greater than growth of construction in the Americas (1.5%).

Comparison with neighbors. The sector of construction in Greenland was less than in Canada ($12.2 billion) and in Iceland ($187.1 million). The sector of construction per capita in Greenland was less than in Iceland ($865.7) and in Canada ($534.7). The growth of construction in Greenland was greater than in Canada (3.3%) and in Iceland (1.6%).

Comparison with leaders. The construction of Greenland was less than in the United States ($81.1 billion), in the USSR ($52.5 billion), in Japan ($43.5 billion), in Germany ($33.8 billion), and in France ($22.4 billion). The sector of construction per capita in Greenland was greater than in the USSR ($208.1); but less than in Germany ($428.6), in France ($417.3), in Japan ($390.8), and in the USA ($371.5). The growth of construction in Greenland was greater than in Japan (3.4%), in France (2.0%), in Germany (0.66%), and in the USA (0.31%); but less than in the USSR (6.5%).

The 1980s

The sector of construction in Greenland was $31.2 million per year in the 1980s, ranked 148th in the world, and was on a par with Laos ($31.5 million). The share in the world was 0.0035%, and 0.012% in the Americas.

The share of construction in the economy of Greenland was 5.0% in the 1980s, ranked 117th in the world, and was on a par with Saint Lucia (5.0%), Nepal (5.0%), Thailand (5.1%).

The construction per capita in Greenland was $590.7 in the 1980s, ranked 35th in the world. The Greenland's construction per capita was greater than construction per capita in the world ($186.2) in 3.2 times, and was greater than construction per capita in the Americas ($396.8) by 48.9%.

The growth of construction in Greenland was 3.1% in the 1980s, ranked 77th in the world, and was on a par with Malaysia (3.1%), Palau (3.1%), Iceland (3.1%). The growth of construction in Greenland (3.1%) was greater than growth of construction in the world (1.7%), was greater than growth of construction in the Americas (0.83%).

Comparison with neighbors. The Greenlandic construction was less than in Canada ($24.2 billion) and in Iceland ($392.8 million). The value added of construction per capita in Greenland was less than in Iceland ($1 635.4) and in Canada ($942.9). The growth of construction in Greenland was greater than in Canada (2.8%); but less than in Iceland (3.1%).

Comparison with leaders. The sector of construction in Greenland was less than in the USA ($180.6 billion), in Japan ($138.7 billion), in the USSR ($72.1 billion), in Germany ($57.8 billion), and in France ($42.5 billion). The construction per capita in Greenland was greater than in the USSR ($262.0); but less than in Japan ($1 143.9), in the United States ($754.4), in France ($751.9), and in Germany ($740.2). The growth of construction in Greenland was greater than in Japan (2.1%), in the USA (1.1%), in France (0.67%), and in Germany (-0.52%); but less than in the USSR (6.2%).

The 1990s

The Greenland's construction was $58.4 million per year in the 1990s, ranked 162nd in the world. The share in the world was 0.0037%, and 0.013% in the Americas.

The share of construction in the economy of Greenland was 5.0% in the 1990s, ranked 127th in the world.

The value of construction per capita in Greenland was $1 046.5 in the 1990s, ranked 32nd in the world, and was on a par with Italy ($1 054.2), Ireland ($1 035.0), Anguilla ($1 028.2). The sector of construction per capita in Greenland was greater than construction per capita in the world ($278.6) in 3.8 times, and was greater than construction per capita in the Americas ($564.1) by 85.5%.

The growth of construction in Greenland was -0.2% in the 1990s, ranked 144th in the world. The growth of construction in Greenland (-0.21%) was less than growth of construction in the world (0.71%), was less than growth of construction in the Americas (1.8%).

Comparison with neighbors. The construction of Greenland was less than in Canada ($31.8 billion) and in Iceland ($578.5 million). The sector of construction per capita in Greenland was less than in Iceland ($2.2 thousand) and in Canada ($1 098.6). The growth of construction in Greenland was greater than in Canada (-0.55%); but less than in Iceland (1.0%).

Comparison with leaders. The value added of construction in Greenland was less than in Japan ($343.2 billion), in the USA ($299.1 billion), in Germany ($125.2 billion), in the UK ($69.8 billion), and in France ($68.8 billion). The sector of construction per capita in Greenland was less than in Japan ($2.7 thousand), in Germany ($1 552.3), in the UK ($1 205.1), in France ($1 158.8), and in the United States ($1 131.2). The growth of construction in Greenland was greater than in the United Kingdom (-0.34%), in France (-0.65%), and in Japan (-1.0%); but less than in the United States (1.8%) and in Germany (-0.047%).

The 2000s

The value of construction in Greenland was $117.7 million per year in the 2000s, ranked 161st in the world, and was on a par with Aruba ($117.3 million), Niger ($119.1 million), Cape Verde ($119.4 million). The share in the world was 0.0047%, and 0.014% in the Americas.

The share of construction in the economy of Greenland was 6.7% in the 2000s, ranked 75th in the world, and was on a par with Uruguay (6.7%).

The sector of construction per capita in Greenland was $2 076.2 in the 2000s, ranked 25th in the world, and was on a par with Finland ($2.1 thousand), Japan ($2.1 thousand), Northern Europe ($2.1 thousand). The Greenlandic construction per capita was greater than construction per capita in the world ($381.3) in 5.4 times, and was greater than construction per capita in the Americas ($931.0) in 2.2 times.

The growth of construction in Greenland was 9.9% in the 2000s, ranked 41st in the world. The growth of construction in Greenland (9.9%) was greater than growth of construction in the world (1.5%), was greater than growth of construction in the Americas (-0.96%).

Comparison with neighbors. The Greenland's construction was less than in Canada ($63.9 billion) and in Iceland ($1.1 billion). The value of construction per capita in Greenland was greater than in Canada ($1 992.6); but less than in Iceland ($3.6 thousand). The growth of construction in Greenland was greater than in Canada (3.6%) and in Iceland (-0.99%).

Comparison with leaders. The construction of Greenland was less than in the USA ($583.0 billion), in Japan ($270.5 billion), in China ($150.1 billion), in the United Kingdom ($132.1 billion), and in Spain ($111.8 billion). The sector of construction per capita in Greenland was greater than in the United States ($1 983.7) and in China ($113.1); but less than in Spain ($2.6 thousand), in the United Kingdom ($2.2 thousand), and in Japan ($2.1 thousand). The growth of construction in Greenland was greater than in Spain (1.7%), in the UK (0.17%), in the United States (-2.6%), and in Japan (-3.9%); but less than in China (11.9%).

The 2010s

The value of construction in Greenland was $259.9 million per year in the 2010s, ranked 160th in the world, and was on a par with

Barbados ($262.2 million), Mozambique ($253.6 million). The share in the world was 0.0062%, and 0.022% in the Americas.

The share of construction in the economy of Greenland was 9.8% in the 2010s, ranked 26th in the world.

The value added of construction per capita in Greenland was $4 600.5 in the 2010s, ranked 7th in the world, and was on a par with Australia ($4.6 thousand), Norway ($4.7 thousand). The value of construction per capita in Greenland was greater than construction per capita in the world ($572.1) in 8.0 times, and was greater than construction per capita in the Americas ($1 189.0) in 3.9 times.

The growth of construction in Greenland was 5.1% in the 2010s, ranked 70th in the world, and was on a par with Northern Africa (5.0%), Nepal (5.1%), Eritrea (5.1%). The growth of construction in Greenland (5.1%) was greater than growth of construction in the world (2.9%), was greater than growth of construction in the Americas (1.3%).

Comparison with neighbors. The value of construction in Greenland was 478.3 times lower than in Canada ($124.3 billion) and 4.0 times lower than in Iceland ($1.0 billion). The construction per capita in Greenland was 32.5% higher than in Canada ($3.5 thousand) and 46.9% higher than in Iceland ($3.1 thousand). The growth of construction in Greenland was greater than in Canada (2.5%); but less than in Iceland (5.9%).

Comparison with leaders. The value of construction in Greenland was 2 812.9 times lower than in China ($731.1 billion), 2 619.3 times lower than in the USA ($680.8 billion), 1 072.1 times lower than in Japan ($278.7 billion), 646.7 times lower than in India ($168.1 billion), and 589.5 times lower than in Germany ($153.2 billion). The value added of construction per capita in Greenland was 2.1 times higher than in Japan ($2.2 thousand), 2.2 times higher than in the United States ($2.1 thousand), 2.5 times higher than in Germany ($1 871.9), 8.8 times higher than in China ($521.3), and 35.6 times higher than in India ($129.1). The growth of construction in Greenland was greater than in Germany (1.8%), in Japan (1.7%), and in the United States (1.4%); but less than in China (8.2%) and in India (5.2%).

Chapter VII. Transportation

Transport, storage and communication (ISIC I)

The sector of transportation in Greenland increased from $28.4 million per year in the 1970s to $327.6 million per year in the 2010s, that is by $299.2 million or 11.5 times. The change occurred at $239.6 million due to a 3.7-fold increase in prices, as also at $55.1 million due to a 2.7-fold increase in productivity, as well as at $4.5 million due to the expansion in population. The average annual growth in transportation is 3.1%. The minimum value of transportation was in 1970 at $9.5 million. The maximum value of transportation was in 2018 at $356.9 million.

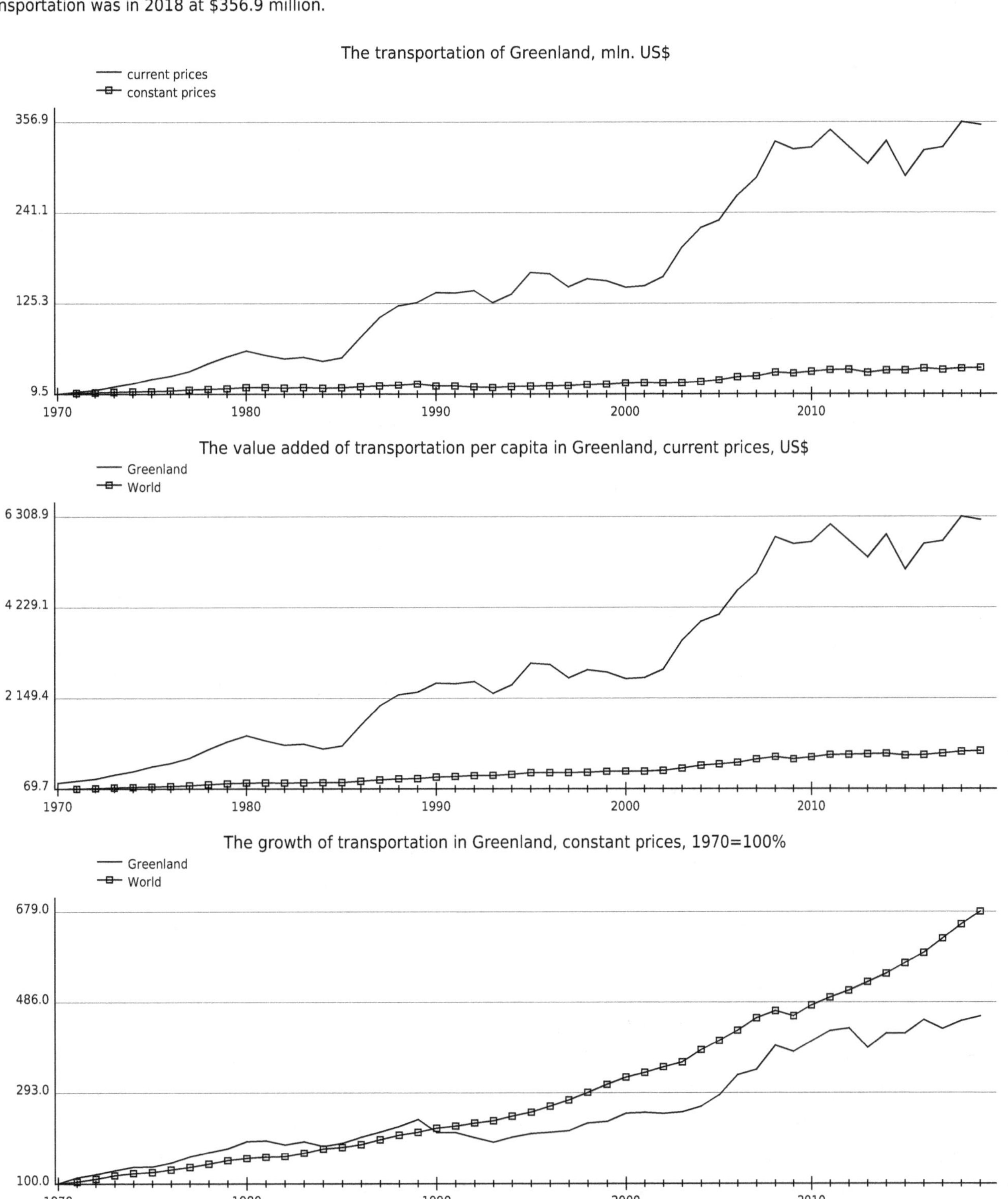

The transportation of Greenland, mln. US$

The value added of transportation per capita in Greenland, current prices, US$

The growth of transportation in Greenland, constant prices, 1970=100%

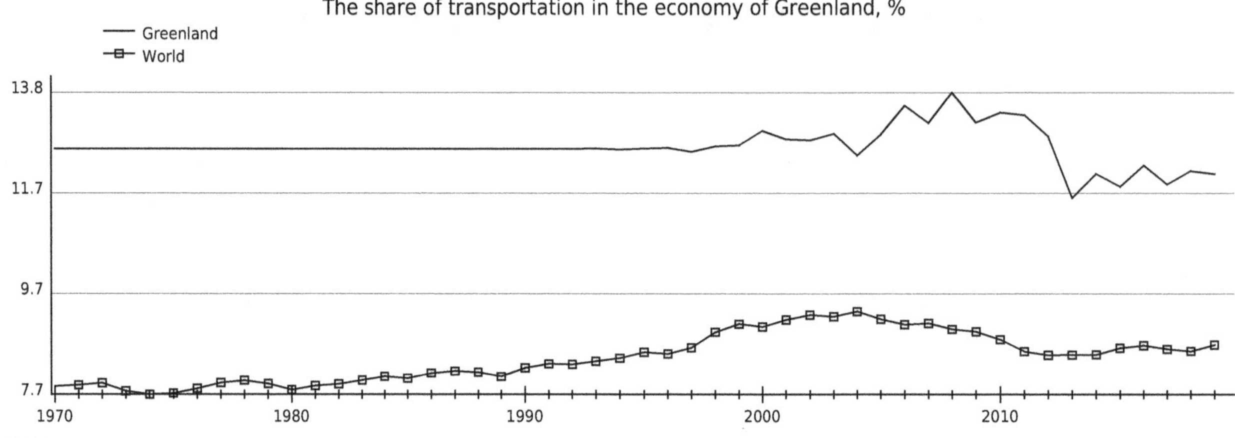

The 1970s

The value of transportation in Greenland was $28.4 million per year in the 1970s, ranked 132nd in the world. The share in the world was 0.0057%, and 0.014% in the Americas.

The share of transportation in the economy of Greenland was 12.6% in the 1970s, ranked 9th in the world, and was on a par with Iceland (12.5%).

The Greenland's transportation per capita was $581.4 in the 1970s, ranked 12th in the world. The value of transportation per capita in Greenland was greater than transportation per capita in the world ($122.3) in 4.8 times, and was greater than transportation per capita in the Americas ($360.9) by 61.1%.

The growth of transportation in Greenland was 6.4% in the 1970s, ranked 74th in the world. The growth of transportation in Greenland (6.4%) was greater than growth of transportation in the world (4.6%), was greater than growth of transportation in the Americas (4.9%).

Comparison with neighbors. The value added of transportation in Greenland was less than in Canada ($12.7 billion) and in Iceland ($167.8 million). The sector of transportation per capita in Greenland was greater than in Canada ($557.0); but less than in Iceland ($776.6). The growth of transportation in Greenland was greater than in Iceland (5.8%) and in Canada (5.7%).

Comparison with leaders. The transportation of Greenland was less than in the USA ($168.6 billion), in Japan ($46.4 billion), in Germany ($29.6 billion), in the USSR ($28.8 billion), and in France ($24.0 billion). The transportation per capita in Greenland was greater than in France ($447.4), in Japan ($416.6), in Germany ($376.1), and in the USSR ($114.0); but less than in the United States ($772.4). The growth of transportation in Greenland was greater than in the United States (4.2%), in France (4.1%), in Germany (3.0%), and in Japan (1.7%); but less than in the USSR (8.1%).

The 1980s

The value added of transportation in Greenland was $78.2 million per year in the 1980s, ranked 126th in the world, and was on a par with Mali ($79.0 million). The share in the world was 0.0067%, and 0.017% in the Americas.

The share of transportation in the economy of Greenland was 12.6% in the 1980s, ranked 16th in the world, and was on a par with Western Africa (12.7%), Saint Lucia (12.7%).

The sector of transportation per capita in Greenland was $1 481.2 in the 1980s, ranked 10th in the world, and was on a par with the UAE ($1 462.8). The value of transportation per capita in Greenland was greater than transportation per capita in the world ($242.0) in 6.1 times, and was greater than transportation per capita in the Americas ($714.8) in 2.1 times.

The growth of transportation in Greenland was 3.1% in the 1980s, ranked 112th in the world, and was on a par with Northern Europe (3.0%). The growth of transportation in Greenland (3.1%) was less than growth of transportation in the world (3.4%), was less than growth of transportation in the Americas (3.5%).

Comparison with neighbors. The value added of transportation in Greenland was less than in Canada ($28.1 billion) and in Iceland ($380.5 million). The transportation per capita in Greenland was greater than in Canada ($1 092.1); but less than in Iceland ($1 583.9). The growth of transportation in Greenland was less than in Canada (3.4%) and in Iceland (3.1%).

Comparison with leaders. The value added of transportation in Greenland was less than in the United States ($394.9 billion), in Japan ($147.7 billion), in Germany ($56.6 billion), in France ($56.2 billion), and in the UK ($53.0 billion). The value added of transportation per capita in Greenland was greater than in Japan ($1 217.8), in France ($993.7), in the UK ($938.7), and in Germany ($725.5); but less than in the United States ($1 649.2). The growth of transportation in Greenland was greater than in the UK (3.0%) and in Germany (1.8%); but less than in France (5.4%), in Japan (4.7%), and in the USA (3.6%).

The 1990s

The Greenland's transportation was $146.6 million per year in the 1990s, ranked 142nd in the world, and was on a par with Chad ($143.5 million). The share in the world was 0.0063%, and 0.017% in the Americas.

The share of transportation in the economy of Greenland was 12.6% in the 1990s, ranked 17th in the world, and was on a par with DR Congo (12.7%), Estonia (12.6%), Tanzania (12.6%).

The Greenlandic transportation per capita was $2 625.0 in the 1990s, ranked 14th in the world, and was on a par with Iceland ($2.6 thousand), Denmark ($2.6 thousand), Singapore ($2.6 thousand). The transportation per capita in Greenland was greater than transportation per capita in the world ($409.5) in 6.4 times, and was greater than transportation per capita in the Americas ($1 104.4) in 2.4 times.

The growth of transportation in Greenland was -0.2% in the 1990s, ranked 176th in the world. The growth of transportation in Greenland (-0.18%) was less than growth of transportation in the world (4.0%), was less than growth of transportation in the Americas (4.7%).

Comparison with neighbors. The transportation of Greenland was less than in Canada ($43.0 billion) and in Iceland ($699.5 million). The sector of transportation per capita in Greenland was greater than in Canada ($1 483.7); but less than in Iceland ($2.6 thousand). The growth of transportation in Greenland was less than in Iceland (6.0%) and in Canada (3.5%).

Comparison with leaders. The sector of transportation in Greenland was less than in the USA ($702.6 billion), in Japan ($373.9 billion), in Germany ($144.3 billion), in France ($118.7 billion), and in the United Kingdom ($117.6 billion). The transportation per capita in Greenland was greater than in the United Kingdom ($2.0 thousand), in France ($1 999.2), and in Germany ($1 789.0); but less than in Japan ($3.0 thousand) and in the USA ($2.7 thousand). The growth of transportation in Greenland was less than in the United States (5.0%), in France (4.8%), in the UK (4.7%), in Germany (3.9%), and in Japan (3.0%).

The 2000s

The value added of transportation in Greenland was $230.5 million per year in the 2000s, ranked 151st in the world, and was on a par with the Cayman Islands ($234.1 million). The share in the world was 0.0057%, and 0.016% in the Americas.

The share of transportation in the economy of Greenland was 13.1% in the 2000s, ranked 18th in the world, and was on a par with Fiji (13.0%), Haiti (13.0%), Pakistan (13.0%).

The value added of transportation per capita in Greenland was $4 066.1 in the 2000s, ranked 10th in the world, and was on a par with the United States ($4.0 thousand), Iceland ($4.0 thousand). The value of transportation per capita in Greenland was greater than transportation per capita in the world ($621.1) in 6.5 times, and was greater than transportation per capita in the Americas ($1 687.7) in 2.4 times.

The growth of transportation in Greenland was 5.1% in the 2000s, ranked 106th in the world, and was on a par with Cape Verde (5.0%), Belize (5.1%). The growth of transportation in Greenland (5.1%) was greater than growth of transportation in the world (3.9%), was greater than growth of transportation in the Americas (3.2%).

Comparison with neighbors. The value of transportation in Greenland was less than in Canada ($78.6 billion) and in Iceland ($1.2 billion). The value added of transportation per capita in Greenland was greater than in Iceland ($4.0 thousand) and in Canada ($2.5 thousand). The growth of transportation in Greenland was greater than in Canada (2.5%) and in Iceland (2.0%).

Comparison with leaders. The sector of transportation in Greenland was less than in the USA ($1.2 trillion), in Japan ($468.5 billion), in Germany ($228.2 billion), in the UK ($215.9 billion), and in France ($185.6 billion). The value added of transportation per capita in Greenland was greater than in the USA ($4.0 thousand), in Japan ($3.7 thousand), in the UK ($3.6 thousand), in France ($3.0 thousand), and in Germany ($2.8 thousand). The growth of transportation in Greenland was greater than in Germany (3.4%), in the United Kingdom (3.1%), in the USA (3.1%), in France (2.7%), and in Japan (1.5%).

The 2010s

The Greenlandic transportation was $327.6 million per year in the 2010s, ranked 164th in the world, and was on a par with Curaçao ($325.6 million), Bermuda ($330.9 million). The share in the world was 0.0052%, and 0.014% in the Americas.

The share of transportation in the economy of Greenland was 12.3% in the 2010s, ranked 25th in the world, and was on a par with Cyprus (12.4%), Eritrea (12.3%), Barbados (12.4%).

The value of transportation per capita in Greenland was $5 798.6 in the 2010s, ranked 8th in the world, and was on a par with Singapore ($5.9 thousand). The transportation per capita in Greenland was greater than transportation per capita in the world ($864.8) in 6.7 times, and was greater than transportation per capita in the Americas ($2 381.9) in 2.4 times.

The growth of transportation in Greenland was 1.8% in the 2010s, ranked 170th in the world, and was on a par with Congo (1.8%). The growth of transportation in Greenland (1.8%) was less than growth of transportation in the world (4.0%), was less than growth of transportation in the Americas (4.7%).

Comparison with neighbors. The value of transportation in Greenland was 365.1 times lower than in Canada ($119.6 billion) and 5.5 times lower than in Iceland ($1.8 billion). The value of transportation per capita in Greenland was 5.5% higher than in Iceland ($5.5 thousand) and 73.6% higher than in Canada ($3.3 thousand). The growth of transportation in Greenland was less than in Iceland (5.9%) and in Canada (2.8%).

Comparison with leaders. The value of transportation in Greenland was 5 459.2 times lower than in the United States ($1.8 trillion), 1 617.3 times lower than in Japan ($529.8 billion), 1 417.1 times lower than in China ($464.2 billion), 915.8 times lower than in Germany ($300.0 billion), and 786.8 times lower than in the UK ($257.7 billion). The Greenlandic transportation per capita was 3.6% higher than in the United States ($5.6 thousand), 40.0% higher than in Japan ($4.1 thousand), 47.6% higher than in the UK ($3.9 thousand), 58.2% higher than in Germany ($3.7 thousand), and 17.5 times higher than in China ($331.0). The growth of transportation in Greenland was greater than in Japan (0.81%); but less than in China (7.5%), in the United States (5.1%), in the United Kingdom (2.8%), and in Germany (2.7%).

Chapter VIII. Trade

Wholesale, retail trade, restaurants and hotels (ISIC G-H)

The value of trade in Greenland grew from $25.8 million per year in the 1970s to $275.9 million per year in the 2010s, that is by $250.1 million or 10.7 times. The change occurred at $226.8 million due to a 5.6-fold increase in prices, as also at $19.2 million due to a 1.6-fold increase in productivity, as well as at $4.0 million due to the expansion in population. The average annual growth in trade is 2.0%. The minimum value of trade was in 1970 at $8.6 million. The maximum value of trade was in 2018 at $333.4 million.

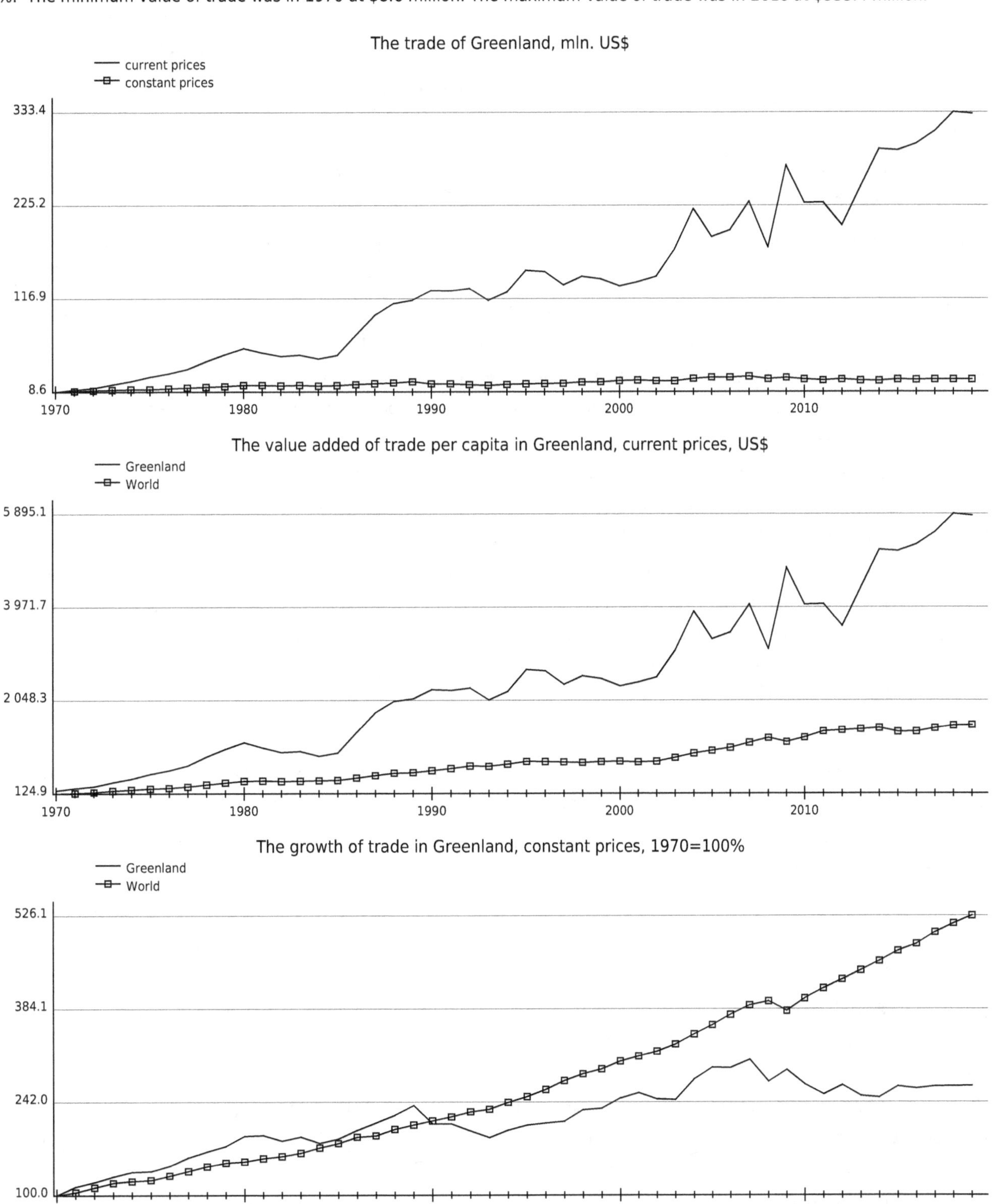

The trade of Greenland, mln. US$

The value added of trade per capita in Greenland, current prices, US$

The growth of trade in Greenland, constant prices, 1970=100%

The 1970s

The trade of Greenland was $25.8 million per year in the 1970s, ranked 152nd in the world. The share in the world was 0.0029%, and 0.0070% in the Americas.

The share of trade in the economy of Greenland was 11.5% in the 1970s, ranked 136th in the world, and was on a par with Dominica (11.5%), Vietnam (11.5%), Australasia (11.4%).

The Greenlandic trade per capita was $528.3 in the 1970s, ranked 38th in the world. The sector of trade per capita in Greenland was greater than trade per capita in the world ($221.0) in 2.4 times, and was less than trade per capita in the Americas ($654.8) by 19.3%.

The growth of trade in Greenland was 6.4% in the 1970s, ranked 59th in the world, and was on a par with Saint Lucia (6.4%), Sudan (6.5%). The growth of trade in Greenland (6.4%) was greater than growth of trade in the world (4.5%), was greater than growth of trade in the Americas (4.4%).

Comparison with neighbors. The sector of trade in Greenland was less than in Canada ($21.5 billion) and in Iceland ($137.6 million). The trade per capita in Greenland was less than in Canada ($942.3) and in Iceland ($636.6). The growth of trade in Greenland was greater than in Canada (5.1%) and in Iceland (4.5%).

Comparison with leaders. The trade of Greenland was less than in the United States ($278.3 billion), in Japan ($90.3 billion), in the USSR ($62.3 billion), in Germany ($61.1 billion), and in France ($40.9 billion). The value of trade per capita in Greenland was greater than in the USSR ($247.1); but less than in the United States ($1 275.1), in Japan ($811.1), in Germany ($775.5), and in France ($762.4). The growth of trade in Greenland was greater than in the USSR (5.2%), in France (3.9%), in the USA (3.9%), and in Germany (3.0%); but less than in Japan (8.2%).

The 1980s

The sector of trade in Greenland was $71.0 million per year in the 1980s, ranked 152nd in the world, and was on a par with Saint Lucia ($70.1 million), Liberia ($69.5 million). The share in the world was 0.0034%, and 0.0085% in the Americas.

The share of trade in the economy of Greenland was 11.5% in the 1980s, ranked 140th in the world, and was on a par with Sweden (11.5%), Mozambique (11.4%).

The value of trade per capita in Greenland was $1 346.0 in the 1980s, ranked 34th in the world, and was on a par with Belgium ($1 355.0). The sector of trade per capita in Greenland was greater than trade per capita in the world ($437.7) in 3.1 times, and was greater than trade per capita in the Americas ($1 268.0) by 6.2%.

The growth of trade in Greenland was 3.1% in the 1980s, ranked 83rd in the world, and was on a par with Botswana (3.0%), Palau (3.1%), Cuba (3.1%). The growth of trade in Greenland (3.1%) was less than growth of trade in the world (3.3%), was less than growth of trade in the Americas (3.5%).

Comparison with neighbors. The trade of Greenland was less than in Canada ($50.0 billion) and in Iceland ($419.0 million). The value added of trade per capita in Greenland was less than in Canada ($1 944.8) and in Iceland ($1 744.3). The growth of trade in Greenland was less than in Canada (3.6%) and in Iceland (3.4%).

Comparison with leaders. The value of trade in Greenland was less than in the USA ($653.3 billion), in Japan ($277.3 billion), in

Germany ($116.7 billion), in the USSR ($112.3 billion), and in Italy ($95.7 billion). The value added of trade per capita in Greenland was greater than in the USSR ($408.1); but less than in the USA ($2.7 thousand), in Japan ($2.3 thousand), in Italy ($1 684.2), and in Germany ($1 496.0). The growth of trade in Greenland was greater than in Italy (2.3%), in Germany (1.8%), and in the USSR (-0.62%); but less than in Japan (4.9%) and in the USA (4.4%).

The 1990s

The sector of trade in Greenland was $133.2 million per year in the 1990s, ranked 169th in the world, and was on a par with Rwanda ($135.7 million), Turkmenistan ($136.3 million). The share in the world was 0.0032%, and 0.0089% in the Americas.

The share of trade in the economy of Greenland was 11.5% in the 1990s, ranked 154th in the world, and was on a par with Hungary (11.5%), Lebanon (11.5%), Fiji (11.4%).

The sector of trade per capita in Greenland was $2 385.6 in the 1990s, ranked 37th in the world, and was on a par with Ireland ($2.4 thousand), Southern Europe ($2.4 thousand), Finland ($2.4 thousand). The trade per capita in Greenland was greater than trade per capita in the world ($721.8) in 3.3 times, and was greater than trade per capita in the Americas ($1 943.2) by 22.8%.

The growth of trade in Greenland was -0.2% in the 1990s, ranked 168th in the world. The growth of trade in Greenland (-0.19%) was less than growth of trade in the world (3.5%), was less than growth of trade in the Americas (3.8%).

Comparison with neighbors. The sector of trade in Greenland was less than in Canada ($76.5 billion) and in Iceland ($879.3 million). The value of trade per capita in Greenland was less than in Iceland ($3.3 thousand) and in Canada ($2.6 thousand). The growth of trade in Greenland was less than in Iceland (3.6%) and in Canada (2.4%).

Comparison with leaders. The value added of trade in Greenland was less than in the USA ($1.2 trillion), in Japan ($713.2 billion), in Germany ($243.7 billion), in Italy ($185.6 billion), and in France ($177.0 billion). The value added of trade per capita in Greenland was less than in Japan ($5.7 thousand), in the United States ($4.4 thousand), in Italy ($3.3 thousand), in Germany ($3.0 thousand), and in France ($3.0 thousand). The growth of trade in Greenland was less than in the United States (4.3%), in Japan (3.8%), in Germany (2.5%), in France (2.4%), and in Italy (1.9%).

The 2000s

The sector of trade in Greenland was $186.8 million per year in the 2000s, ranked 175th in the world, and was on a par with the Central African Republic ($188.2 million), the TCI ($184.5 million). The share in the world was 0.0029%, and 0.0077% in the Americas.

The share of trade in the economy of Greenland was 10.6% in the 2000s, ranked 180th in the world, and was on a par with Somalia (10.6%), the Cayman Islands (10.7%), Puerto Rico (10.7%).

The sector of trade per capita in Greenland was $3 294.2 in the 2000s, ranked 40th in the world, and was on a par with Antigua and Barbuda ($3.3 thousand). The value added of trade per capita in Greenland was greater than trade per capita in the world ($990.3) in 3.3 times, and was greater than trade per capita in the Americas ($2 770.2) by 18.9%.

The growth of trade in Greenland was 2.3% in the 2000s, ranked 142nd in the world, and was on a par with Fiji (2.3%). The growth of trade in Greenland (2.3%) was less than growth of trade in the world (2.7%), was greater than growth of trade in the Americas (1.6%).

Comparison with neighbors. The trade of Greenland was less than in Canada ($129.8 billion) and in Iceland ($1.4 billion). The value added of trade per capita in Greenland was less than in Iceland ($4.7 thousand) and in Canada ($4.0 thousand). The growth of trade in Greenland was greater than in Iceland (1.5%); but less than in Canada (2.9%).

Comparison with leaders. The trade of Greenland was less than in the United States ($1.9 trillion), in Japan ($771.8 billion), in Germany ($296.0 billion), in the UK ($293.5 billion), and in China ($262.0 billion). The sector of trade per capita in Greenland was greater than in China ($197.5); but less than in the United States ($6.4 thousand), in Japan ($6.0 thousand), in the United Kingdom ($4.9 thousand), and in Germany ($3.6 thousand). The growth of trade in Greenland was greater than in Germany (1.7%), in the United Kingdom (1.3%), in the United States (1.1%), and in Japan (-0.77%); but less than in China (11.9%).

The 2010s

The value of trade in Greenland was $275.9 million per year in the 2010s, ranked 180th in the world. The share in the world was 0.0026%, and 0.0074% in the Americas.

The share of trade in the economy of Greenland was 10.4% in the 2010s, ranked 183rd in the world.

The trade per capita in Greenland was \$4 882.9 in the 2010s, ranked 35th in the world, and was on a par with Spain (\$4.9 thousand), Anguilla (\$5.0 thousand). The trade per capita in Greenland was greater than trade per capita in the world (\$1 436.8) in 3.4 times, and was greater than trade per capita in the Americas (\$3 802.7) by 28.4%.

The growth of trade in Greenland was -0.9% in the 2010s, ranked 195th in the world. The growth of trade in Greenland (-0.87%) was less than growth of trade in the world (3.3%), was less than growth of trade in the Americas (2.1%).

Comparison with neighbors. The Greenland's trade was 724.2 times lower than in Canada (\$199.8 billion) and 7.5 times lower than in Iceland (\$2.1 billion). The value added of trade per capita in Greenland was 22.1% lower than in Iceland (\$6.3 thousand) and 12.5% lower than in Canada (\$5.6 thousand). The growth of trade in Greenland was less than in Iceland (5.3%) and in Canada (2.5%).

Comparison with leaders. The sector of trade in Greenland was 9 481.0 times lower than in the United States (\$2.6 trillion), 4 329.6 times lower than in China (\$1.2 trillion), 3 152.0 times lower than in Japan (\$869.5 billion), 1 350.7 times lower than in Germany (\$372.6 billion), and 1 196.2 times lower than in the United Kingdom (\$330.0 billion). The sector of trade per capita in Greenland was 7.3% higher than in Germany (\$4.6 thousand) and 5.7 times higher than in China (\$851.7); but 40.4% lower than in the USA (\$8.2 thousand), 28.2% lower than in Japan (\$6.8 thousand), and 2.9% lower than in the UK (\$5.0 thousand). The growth of trade in Greenland was less than in China (8.9%), in the UK (2.8%), in the USA (2.3%), in Germany (2.0%), and in Japan (0.77%).

Chapter IX. Services

(ISIC J-P)

The value of services in Greenland rose from $96.7 million per year in the 1970s to $1.1 billion per year in the 2010s, that is by $1.0 billion or 11.4 times. The change occurred at $912.9 million due to a 5.7-fold increase in prices, as also at $81.0 million due to a 1.7-fold increase in productivity, as well as at $15.2 million due to the growth in population. The average annual growth in services is 2.1%. The minimum value of services was in 1970 at $32.2 million. The maximum value of services was in 2014 at $1.2 billion.

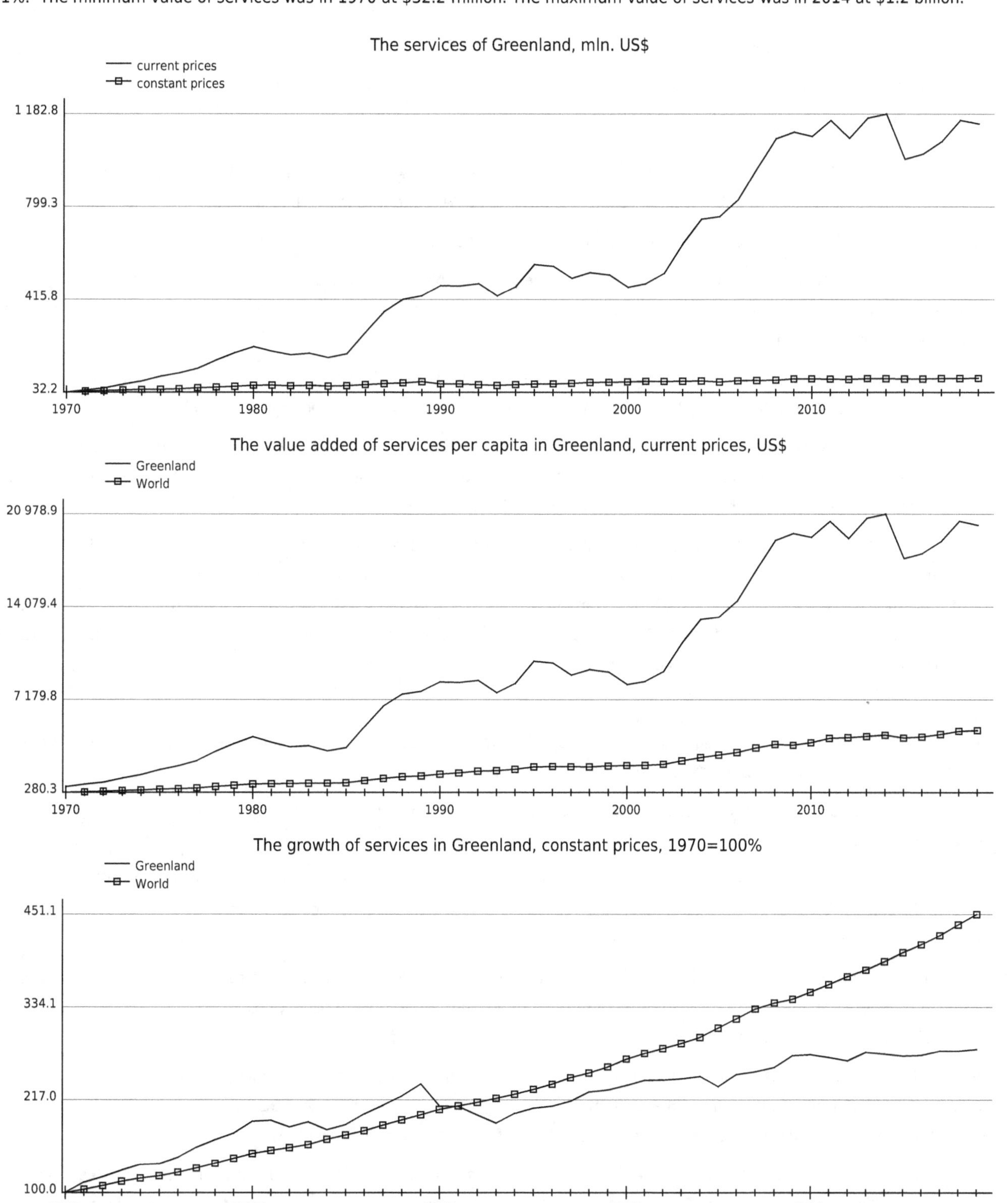

The services of Greenland, mln. US$

The value added of services per capita in Greenland, current prices, US$

The growth of services in Greenland, constant prices, 1970=100%

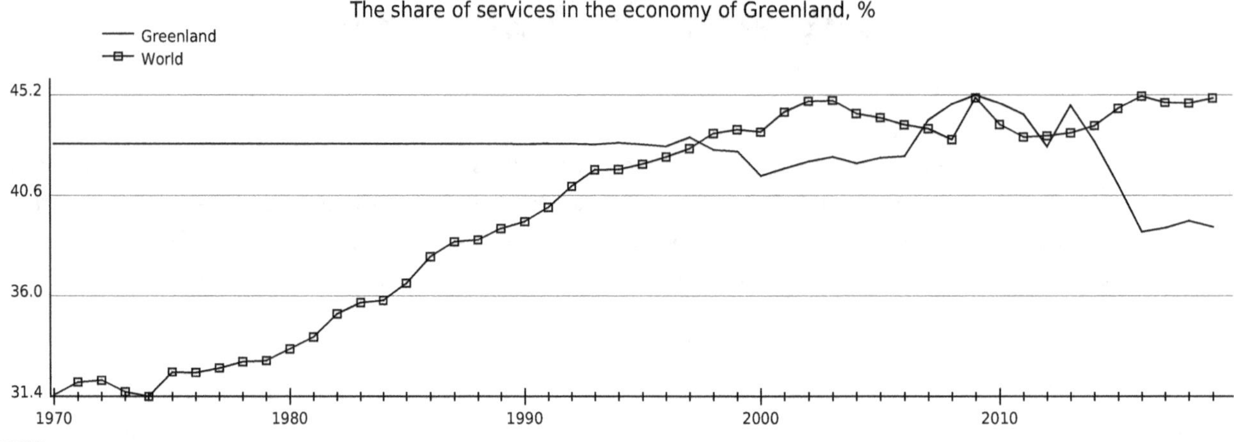

The 1970s

The value of services in Greenland was $96.7 million per year in the 1970s, ranked 141st in the world, and was on a par with Brunei ($96.9 million), Swaziland ($97.7 million). The share in the world was 0.0047%, and 0.011% in the Americas.

The share of services in the economy of Greenland was 43.0% in the 1970s, ranked 18th in the world.

The value of services per capita in Greenland was $1 979.4 in the 1970s, ranked 22nd in the world, and was on a par with Belgium ($1 980.8). The Greenland's services per capita were greater than services per capita in the world ($506.9) in 3.9 times, and were greater than services per capita in the Americas ($1 502.8) by 31.7%.

The growth of services in Greenland was 6.4% in the 1970s, ranked 67th in the world. The growth of services in Greenland (6.4%) was greater than growth of services in the world (4.1%), was greater than growth of services in the Americas (3.7%).

Comparison with neighbors. The services of Greenland were less than in Canada ($57.1 billion) and in Iceland ($393.3 million). The value of services per capita in Greenland was greater than in Iceland ($1 820.1); but less than in Canada ($2.5 thousand). The growth of services in Greenland was greater than in Iceland (6.3%) and in Canada (4.0%).

Comparison with leaders. The sector of services in Greenland was less than in the United States ($674.4 billion), in the USSR ($168.3 billion), in Japan ($153.8 billion), in Germany ($150.2 billion), and in France ($121.8 billion). The value added of services per capita in Greenland was greater than in Germany ($1 907.6), in Japan ($1 381.3), and in the USSR ($667.3); but less than in the United States ($3.1 thousand) and in France ($2.3 thousand). The growth of services in Greenland was greater than in Japan (5.9%), in Germany (4.8%), in France (3.9%), in the USA (3.3%), and in the USSR (0.90%).

The 1980s

The services of Greenland were $266.2 million per year in the 1980s, ranked 136th in the world, and were on a par with Liberia ($259.9 million). The share in the world was 0.0049%, and 0.012% in the Americas.

The share of services in the economy of Greenland was 43.0% in the 1980s, ranked 27th in the world, and was on a par with Djibouti (43.2%), the UK (42.7%), Dominica (42.7%).

The Greenlandic services per capita were $5 042.7 in the 1980s, ranked 21st in the world, and were on a par with Western Europe ($5.0 thousand), Japan ($5.1 thousand), Australasia ($4.9 thousand). The Greenland's services per capita were greater than services per capita in the world ($1 115.5) in 4.5 times, and were greater than services per capita in the Americas ($3 456.8) by 45.9%.

The growth of services in Greenland was 3.1% in the 1980s, ranked 105th in the world, and was on a par with Mexico (3.1%), Germany (3.1%), Djibouti (3.1%). The growth of services in Greenland (3.1%) was less than growth of services in the world (3.3%), was greater than growth of services in the Americas (2.8%).

Comparison with neighbors. The value of services in Greenland was less than in Canada ($147.0 billion) and in Iceland ($1.1 billion). The Greenland's services per capita were greater than in Iceland ($4.7 thousand); but less than in Canada ($5.7 thousand). The growth of services in Greenland was greater than in Canada (2.8%); but less than in Iceland (4.8%).

Comparison with leaders. The sector of services in Greenland was less than in the USA ($1.9 trillion), in Japan ($619.9 billion), in Germany ($362.2 billion), in France ($294.5 billion), and in the United Kingdom ($265.4 billion). The sector of services per capita in

Greenland was greater than in the United Kingdom ($4.7 thousand) and in Germany ($4.6 thousand); but less than in the USA ($7.8 thousand), in France ($5.2 thousand), and in Japan ($5.1 thousand). The growth of services in Greenland was greater than in the USA (2.8%) and in France (2.3%); but less than in Japan (4.8%), in the UK (3.3%), and in Germany (3.1%).

The 1990s

The sector of services in Greenland was $498.1 million per year in the 1990s, ranked 147th in the world, and was on a par with Moldova ($502.4 million), Benin ($509.7 million). The share in the world was 0.0043%, and 0.010% in the Americas.

The share of services in the economy of Greenland was 42.9% in the 1990s, ranked 42nd in the world, and was on a par with Montserrat (43.0%), Europe (43.1%), Uruguay (43.1%).

The services per capita in Greenland were $8 919.9 in the 1990s, ranked 25th in the world, and were on a par with Macao ($9.0 thousand), Austria ($9.0 thousand), Australia ($8.8 thousand). The value added of services per capita in Greenland was greater than services per capita in the world ($2 014.6) in 4.4 times, and was greater than services per capita in the Americas ($6 173.1) by 44.5%.

The growth of services in Greenland was -0.3% in the 1990s, ranked 181st in the world, and was on a par with the Marshall Islands (-0.32%). The growth of services in Greenland (-0.32%) was less than growth of services in the world (2.7%), was less than growth of services in the Americas (2.4%).

Comparison with neighbors. The value added of services in Greenland was less than in Canada ($266.4 billion) and in Iceland ($2.3 billion). The value of services per capita in Greenland was greater than in Iceland ($8.6 thousand); but less than in Canada ($9.2 thousand). The growth of services in Greenland was less than in Iceland (3.5%) and in Canada (2.5%).

Comparison with leaders. The services of Greenland were less than in the United States ($3.8 trillion), in Japan ($1.6 trillion), in Germany ($908.0 billion), in France ($628.2 billion), and in the United Kingdom ($592.3 billion). The services per capita in Greenland were less than in the United States ($14.4 thousand), in Japan ($12.8 thousand), in Germany ($11.3 thousand), in France ($10.6 thousand), and in the United Kingdom ($10.2 thousand). The growth of services in Greenland was less than in Germany (3.2%), in the UK (3.0%), in the USA (2.3%), in Japan (1.7%), and in France (1.6%).

The 2000s

The sector of services in Greenland was $759.5 million per year in the 2000s, ranked 157th in the world, and was on a par with Montenegro ($755.4 million). The share in the world was 0.0039%, and 0.0092% in the Americas.

The share of services in the economy of Greenland was 43.2% in the 2000s, ranked 48th in the world, and was on a par with Dominica (43.1%).

The value added of services per capita in Greenland was $13 395.8 in the 2000s, ranked 29th in the world, and was on a par with Macao ($13.6 thousand), Austria ($13.7 thousand). The services per capita in Greenland were greater than services per capita in the world ($3 011.2) in 4.4 times, and were greater than services per capita in the Americas ($9 407.5) by 42.4%.

The growth of services in Greenland was 1.8% in the 2000s, ranked 178th in the world, and was on a par with Barbados (1.8%). The growth of services in Greenland (1.8%) was less than growth of services in the world (2.9%), was less than growth of services in the Americas (2.2%).

Comparison with neighbors. The Greenland's services were less than in Canada ($491.7 billion) and in Iceland ($5.8 billion). The value of services per capita in Greenland was less than in Iceland ($19.5 thousand) and in Canada ($15.3 thousand). The growth of services in Greenland was less than in Iceland (4.2%) and in Canada (3.0%).

Comparison with leaders. The services of Greenland were less than in the USA ($6.7 trillion), in Japan ($2.0 trillion), in Germany ($1.2 trillion), in the UK ($1.1 trillion), and in France ($997.0 billion). The Greenland's services per capita were less than in the United States ($22.9 thousand), in the United Kingdom ($18.0 thousand), in France ($15.9 thousand), in Japan ($15.3 thousand), and in Germany ($15.0 thousand). The growth of services in Greenland was greater than in France (1.5%), in Japan (1.2%), and in Germany (0.57%); but less than in the United Kingdom (2.7%) and in the USA (2.0%).

The 2010s

The value of services in Greenland was $1.1 billion per year in the 2010s, ranked 168th in the world, and was on a par with Tajikistan ($1.1 billion). The share in the world was 0.0034%, and 0.0086% in the Americas.

The share of services in the economy of Greenland was 41.7% in the 2010s, ranked 69th in the world, and was on a par with South Korea (41.8%), Bahrain (41.6%), Georgia (41.6%).

The services per capita in Greenland were $19 572.0 in the 2010s, ranked 27th in the world, and were on a par with Germany ($19.6 thousand), Finland ($19.8 thousand), Andorra ($20.1 thousand). The value added of services per capita in Greenland was greater than services per capita in the world ($4 467.8) in 4.4 times, and was greater than services per capita in the Americas ($13 184.6) by 48.4%.

The growth of services in Greenland was 0.3% in the 2010s, ranked 191st in the world. The growth of services in Greenland (0.29%) was less than growth of services in the world (2.7%), was less than growth of services in the Americas (1.8%).

Comparison with neighbors. The Greenlandic services were 737.5 times lower than in Canada ($815.5 billion) and 7.5 times lower than in Iceland ($8.3 billion). The Greenlandic services per capita were 21.8% lower than in Iceland ($25.0 thousand) and 14.0% lower than in Canada ($22.8 thousand). The growth of services in Greenland was less than in Canada (2.2%) and in Iceland (1.7%).

Comparison with leaders. The value added of services in Greenland was 9 003.0 times lower than in the USA ($10.0 trillion), 3 207.8 times lower than in China ($3.5 trillion), 2 056.1 times lower than in Japan ($2.3 trillion), 1 453.7 times lower than in Germany ($1.6 trillion), and 1 225.9 times lower than in the UK ($1.4 trillion). The services per capita in Greenland were 10.1% higher than in Japan ($17.8 thousand) and 7.7 times higher than in China ($2.5 thousand); but 37.2% lower than in the United States ($31.2 thousand), 5.3% lower than in the UK ($20.7 thousand), and 0.33% lower than in Germany ($19.6 thousand). The growth of services in Greenland was less than in China (8.4%), in the United States (1.8%), in the United Kingdom (1.7%), in Germany (1.2%), and in Japan (0.99%).

Part III. External relations

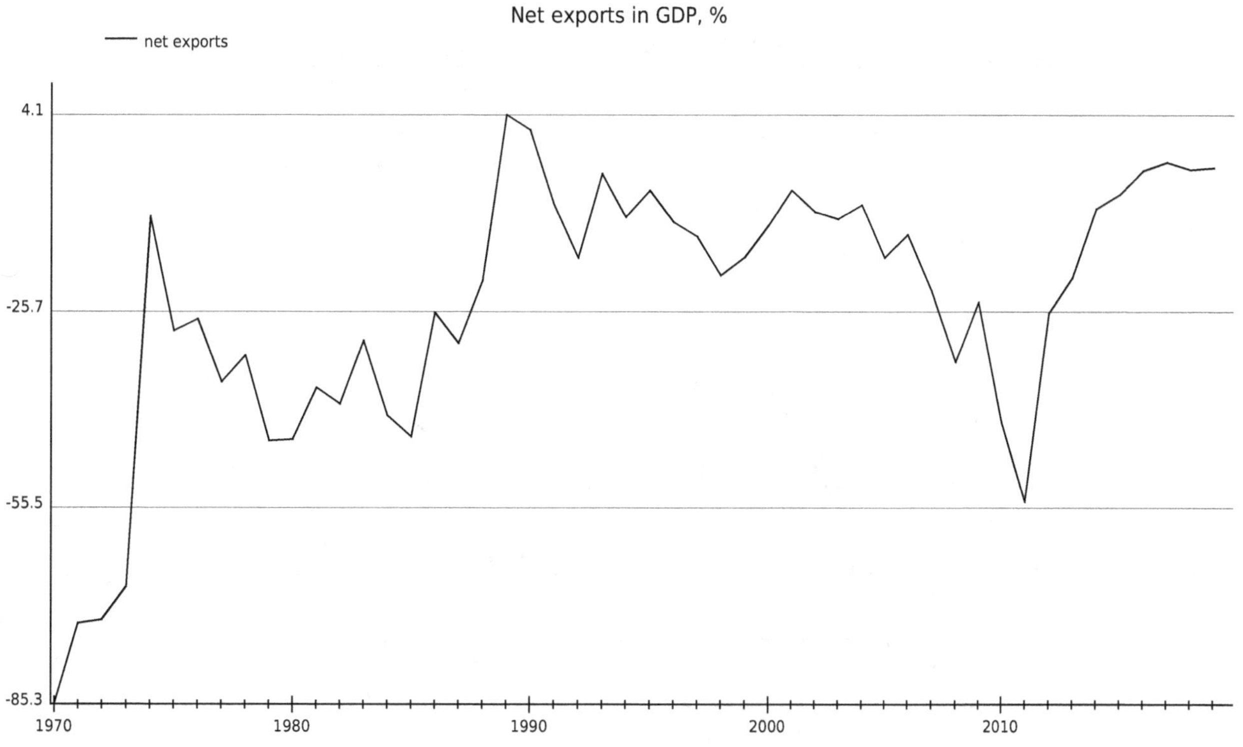

Chapter X. Exports

Exports of goods and services

The Greenland's exports enlarged from $117.9 million per year in the 1970s to $1.1 billion per year in the 2010s, that is by $945.8 million or 9.0 times. The change occurred at $849.5 million due to a 5.0-fold increase in prices, as also at $77.8 million due to a 1.6-fold increase in per capita rate, as well as at $18.5 million due to the rise in population. The average annual growth in exports is 3.1%. The minimum value of exports was in 1970 at $23.8 million. The maximum value of exports was in 2018 at $1.2 billion.

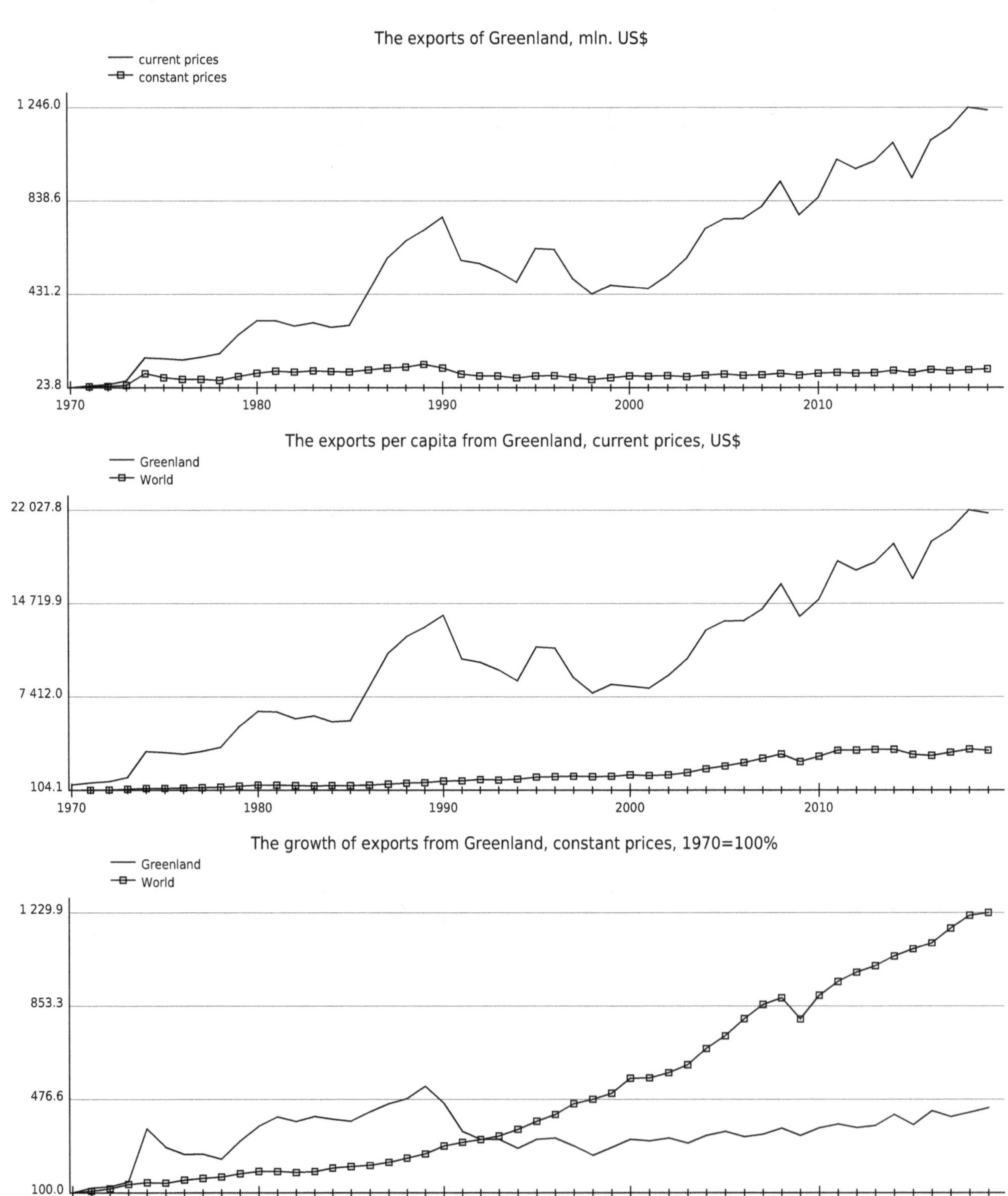

The exports of Greenland, mln. US$

The exports per capita from Greenland, current prices, US$

The growth of exports from Greenland, constant prices, 1970=100%

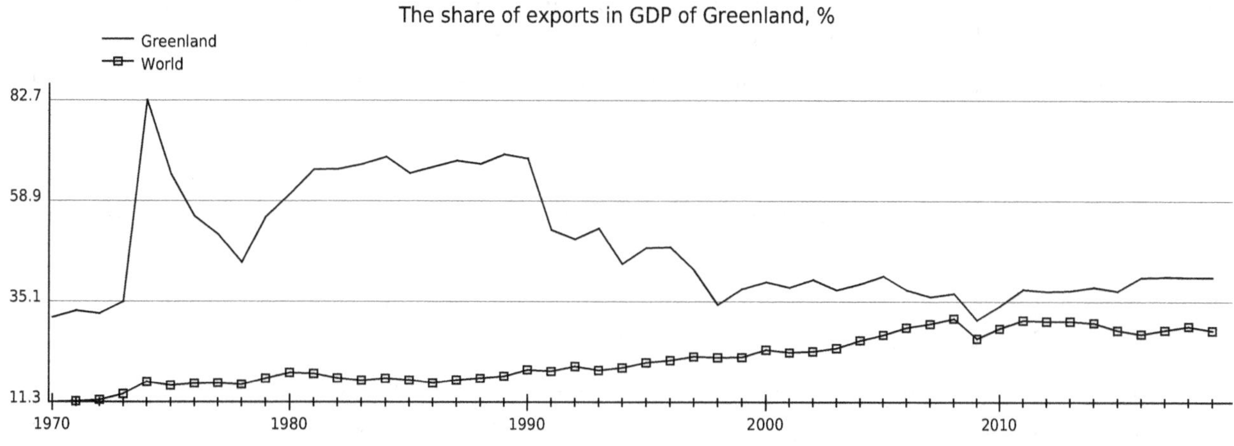

The 1970s

The Greenland's exports were $117.9 million per year in the 1970s, ranked 139th in the world, and were on a par with Botswana ($118.6 million). The share in the world was 0.012%, and 0.053% from the Americas.

The share of exports in GDP of Greenland was 51.7% in the 1970s, ranked 34th in the world, and was on a par with Oman (51.7%), Trinidad and Tobago (52.2%).

The exports per capita from Greenland were $2 413.4 in the 1970s, ranked 22nd in the world, and were on a par with Nauru ($2.4 thousand). The exports per capita from Greenland were greater than exports per capita in the world ($242.1) in 10.0 times, and were greater than exports per capita from the Americas ($397.2) in 6.1 times.

The growth of exports from Greenland was 13.3% in the 1970s, ranked 14th in the world, and was on a par with Nepal (13.2%), the Virgin Islands (13.2%), Lesotho (13.3%). The growth of exports from Greenland (13.3%) was greater than growth of exports in the world (6.5%), was greater than growth of exports from the Americas (6.4%).

Comparison with neighbors. The exports of Greenland were less than from Canada ($38.2 billion) and from Iceland ($535.8 million). The value of exports per capita from Greenland was greater than from Canada ($1 673.2); but less than from Iceland ($2.5 thousand). The growth of exports from Greenland was greater than from Iceland (6.2%) and from Canada (4.1%).

Comparison with leaders. The exports of Greenland were less than from the USA ($128.0 billion), from Germany ($82.9 billion), from France ($64.3 billion), from Japan ($64.1 billion), and from the United Kingdom ($61.3 billion). The value of exports per capita from Greenland was greater than from France ($1 199.1), from the United Kingdom ($1 094.1), from Germany ($1 052.2), from the USA ($586.5), and from Japan ($575.8). The growth of exports from Greenland was greater than from Japan (8.6%), from France (7.8%), from the USA (6.8%), from Germany (5.1%), and from the United Kingdom (5.0%).

The 1980s

The exports of Greenland were $421.6 million per year in the 1980s, ranked 122nd in the world, and were on a par with Albania ($429.9 million). The share in the world was 0.016%, and 0.071% from the Americas.

The share of exports in GDP of Greenland was 67.2% in the 1980s, ranked 20th in the world.

The Greenlandic exports per capita were $7 987.4 in the 1980s, ranked 14th in the world. The exports per capita from Greenland were greater than exports per capita in the world ($529.9) in 15.1 times, and were greater than exports per capita from the Americas ($890.9) in 9.0 times.

The growth of exports from Greenland was 5.5% in the 1980s, ranked 55th in the world. The growth of exports from Greenland (5.5%) was greater than growth of exports in the world (3.8%), was greater than growth of exports from the Americas (5.1%).

Comparison with neighbors. The exports of Greenland were less than from Canada ($101.1 billion) and from Iceland ($1.4 billion). The Greenland's exports per capita were greater than from Iceland ($5.8 thousand) and from Canada ($3.9 thousand). The growth of exports from Greenland was greater than from Canada (4.7%) and from Iceland (2.8%).

Comparison with leaders. The value of exports from Greenland was less than from the USA ($338.6 billion), from Japan ($210.6 billion), from Germany ($208.1 billion), from France ($155.9 billion), and from the United Kingdom ($155.0 billion). The value of exports per capita from Greenland was greater than from France ($2.8 thousand), from the United Kingdom ($2.7 thousand), from Germany ($2.7 thousand), from Japan ($1 736.5), and from the USA ($1 413.8). The growth of exports from Greenland was greater than from Germany (4.7%), from France (4.0%), and from the United Kingdom (3.0%); but less than from Japan (6.7%) and from the United States (5.7%).

The 1990s

The exports of Greenland were $558.4 million per year in the 1990s, ranked 146th in the world, and were on a par with Sudan ($549.6 million), Mauritania ($545.4 million), Guinea ($572.6 million). The share in the world was 0.0095%, and 0.044% from the Americas.

The share of exports in GDP of Greenland was 47.5% in the 1990s, ranked 52nd in the world, and was on a par with Brunei (47.6%), Gambia (47.2%), the Caribbean (47.7%).

The Greenlandic exports per capita were $9 999.7 in the 1990s, ranked 21st in the world, and were on a par with Sweden ($10.1 thousand). The exports per capita from Greenland were greater than exports per capita in the world ($1 029.5) in 9.7 times, and were greater than exports per capita from the Americas ($1 662.5) in 6.0 times.

The growth of exports from Greenland was -6.1% in the 1990s, ranked 193rd in the world. The growth of exports from Greenland (-6.1%) was less than growth of exports in the world (6.9%), was less than growth of exports from the Americas (7.3%).

Comparison with neighbors. The Greenland's exports were less than from Canada ($205.3 billion) and from Iceland ($2.4 billion). The Greenland's exports per capita were greater than from Iceland ($9.1 thousand) and from Canada ($7.1 thousand). The growth of exports from Greenland was less than from Canada (8.0%) and from Iceland (2.2%).

Comparison with leaders. The exports of Greenland were less than from the United States ($773.6 billion), from Germany ($509.0 billion), from Japan ($418.7 billion), from France ($329.8 billion), and from the United Kingdom ($324.3 billion). The Greenlandic exports per capita were greater than from Germany ($6.3 thousand), from the United Kingdom ($5.6 thousand), from France ($5.6 thousand), from Japan ($3.3 thousand), and from the United States ($2.9 thousand). The growth of exports from Greenland was less than from the USA (7.2%), from France (6.5%), from Germany (6.0%), from the UK (5.7%), and from Japan (4.2%).

The 2000s

The exports of Greenland were $677.5 million per year in the 2000s, ranked 169th in the world, and were on a par with Lesotho ($669.5 million), North Korea ($690.6 million). The share in the world was 0.0054%, and 0.028% from the Americas.

The structure of exports: primary products (57.7%), resource-based manufactures (33.0%), and medium technology manufactures (1.6%).

Greenland exported goods to Denmark (86.9%), Canada (2.5%), Spain (2.2%), the United States (1.6%), the United Kingdom (1.1%) and other countries (5.6%).

The share of exports in GDP of Greenland was 37.3% in the 2000s, ranked 98th in the world, and was on a par with South Korea (37.4%), the Bahamas (37.4%), Jamaica (37.5%).

The exports per capita from Greenland were $11 948.5 in the 2000s, ranked 35th in the world, and were on a par with Curaçao ($12.0 thousand). The Greenland's exports per capita were greater than exports per capita in the world ($1 933.7) in 6.2 times, and were greater than exports per capita from the Americas ($2 781.7) in 4.3 times.

The growth of exports from Greenland was 1.6% in the 2000s, ranked 163rd in the world. The growth of exports from Greenland (1.6%) was less than growth of exports in the world (4.8%), was less than growth of exports from the Americas (2.9%).

Comparison with neighbors. The Greenland's exports were less than from Canada ($398.6 billion) and from Iceland ($4.9 billion). The Greenland's exports per capita were less than from Iceland ($16.5 thousand) and from Canada ($12.4 thousand). The growth of exports from Greenland was greater than from Canada (-0.37%); but less than from Iceland (5.8%).

Comparison with leaders. The Greenland's exports were less than from the USA ($1.3 trillion), from Germany ($1.0 trillion), from China ($780.2 billion), from Japan ($626.3 billion), and from the UK ($591.1 billion). The exports per capita from Greenland were greater than from the UK ($9.8 thousand), from Japan ($4.9 thousand), from the USA ($4.5 thousand), and from China ($588.1); but less than from Germany ($12.8 thousand). The growth of exports from Greenland was less than from China (12.7%), from Germany (5.0%), from Japan (3.5%), from the USA (3.3%), and from the UK (2.8%).

The 2010s

The value of exports from Greenland was $1.1 billion per year in the 2010s, ranked 174th in the world, and was on a par with Lesotho ($1.0 billion). The share in the world was 0.0047%, and 0.026% from the Americas.

The structure of exports: primary products (66.0%), resource-based manufactures (24.0%), and medium technology manufactures (4.4%).

Greenland exported goods to Denmark (88.6%), Portugal (4.1%), Iceland (3.2%), Taiwan (1.1%), Switzerland (0.67%) and other countries (2.3%).

The share of exports in GDP of Greenland was 38.8% in the 2010s, ranked 98th in the world, and was on a par with Namibia (38.9%), Norway (38.7%), Central Asia (38.6%).

The Greenland's exports per capita were $18 827.1 in the 2010s, ranked 31st in the world, and were on a par with Northern Europe ($18.7 thousand). The Greenlandic exports per capita were greater than exports per capita in the world ($3 098.9) in 6.1 times, and were greater than exports per capita from the Americas ($4 197.2) in 4.5 times.

The growth of exports from Greenland was 3% in the 2010s, ranked 136th in the world, and was on a par with New Zealand (2.9%), Nepal (2.9%), the Bahamas (3.0%). The growth of exports from Greenland (3.0%) was less than growth of exports in the world (4.4%), was less than growth of exports from the Americas (3.6%).

Comparison with neighbors. The exports of Greenland were 500.0 times lower than from Canada ($531.8 billion) and 8.9 times lower than from Iceland ($9.5 billion). The Greenland's exports per capita were 26.8% higher than from Canada ($14.8 thousand); but 34.3% lower than from Iceland ($28.7 thousand). The growth of exports from Greenland was less than from Iceland (3.9%) and from Canada (3.4%).

Comparison with leaders. The Greenland's exports were 2 156.1 times lower than from China ($2.3 trillion), 2 133.8 times lower than from the United States ($2.3 trillion), 1 582.5 times lower than from Germany ($1.7 trillion), 808.0 times lower than from Japan ($859.4 billion), and 766.3 times lower than from the United Kingdom ($815.1 billion). The exports per capita from Greenland were 51.5% higher than from the UK ($12.4 thousand), 2.7 times higher than from the USA ($7.1 thousand), 2.8 times higher than from Japan ($6.7 thousand), and 11.5 times higher than from China ($1 635.3); but 8.4% lower than from Germany ($20.6 thousand). The growth of exports from Greenland was less than from China (6.8%), from Germany (4.7%), from Japan (4.6%), from the United States (3.7%), and from the United Kingdom (3.1%).

Chapter XI. Imports

Imports of goods and services

The value of imports in Greenland grew up from $210.5 million per year in the 1970s to $1.5 billion per year in the 2010s, that is by $1.3 billion or 7.3 times. The change occurred at $1.2 billion due to a 5.3-fold increase in prices, as also at $46.6 million due to a 1.2-fold increase in per capita rate, as well as at $33.0 million due to the growing in population. The average annual growth in imports is 0.88%. The minimum value of imports was in 1970 at $88.5 million. The maximum value of imports was in 2011 at $2.5 billion.

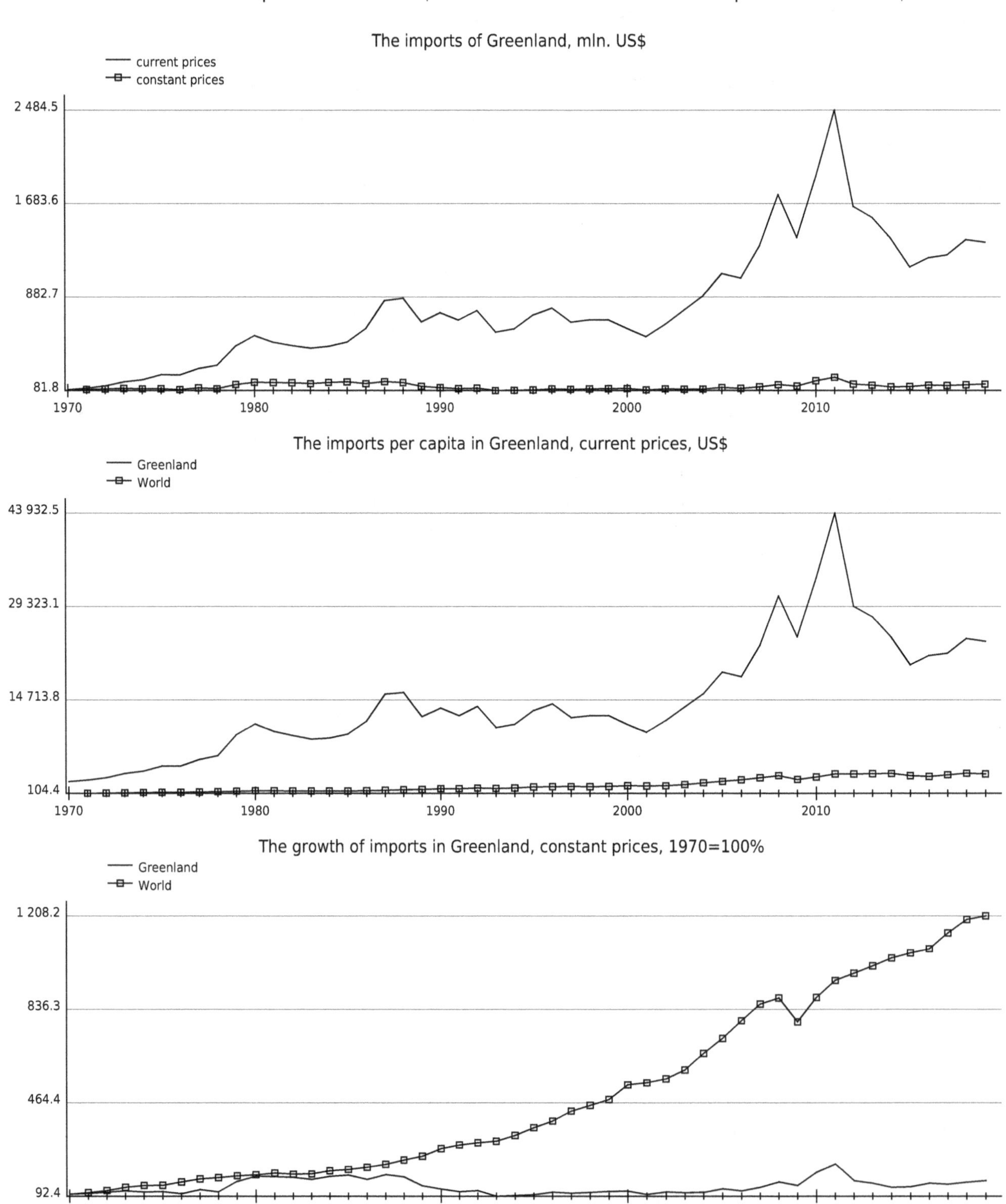

The imports of Greenland, mln. US$

The imports per capita in Greenland, current prices, US$

The growth of imports in Greenland, constant prices, 1970=100%

The 1970s

The imports of Greenland were $210.5 million per year in the 1970s, ranked 136th in the world, and were on a par with Guyana ($214.2 million). The share in the world was 0.021%, and 0.089% in the Americas.

The share of imports in GDP of Greenland was 92.4% in the 1970s, ranked 9th in the world, and was on a par with Panama (92.8%).

The value of imports per capita in Greenland was $4 310.5 in the 1970s, ranked 9th in the world. The value of imports per capita in Greenland was greater than imports per capita in the world ($244.3) in 17.6 times, and was greater than imports per capita in the Americas ($421.7) in 10.2 times.

The growth of imports in Greenland was 4.7% in the 1970s, ranked 111th in the world, and was on a par with Italy (4.6%), Vietnam (4.7%), the Caribbean (4.7%). The growth of imports in Greenland (4.7%) was less than growth of imports in the world (6.3%), was less than growth of imports in the Americas (5.4%).

Comparison with neighbors. The Greenlandic imports were less than in Canada ($38.2 billion) and in Iceland ($561.3 million). The Greenland's imports per capita were greater than in Iceland ($2.6 thousand) and in Canada ($1 670.3). The growth of imports in Greenland was less than in Iceland (6.9%) and in Canada (6.4%).

Comparison with leaders. The imports of Greenland were less than in the United States ($133.2 billion), in Germany ($92.5 billion), in France ($63.3 billion), in the United Kingdom ($62.4 billion), and in Japan ($61.0 billion). The value of imports per capita in Greenland was greater than in France ($1 181.1), in Germany ($1 175.1), in the UK ($1 113.2), in the United States ($610.4), and in Japan ($547.6). The growth of imports in Greenland was greater than in the UK (4.5%); but less than in France (7.2%), in Japan (7.0%), in Germany (5.6%), and in the USA (5.1%).

The 1980s

The value of imports in Greenland was $591.2 million per year in the 1980s, ranked 123rd in the world, and was on a par with El Salvador ($586.6 million), Nepal ($596.4 million), Niger ($598.5 million). The share in the world was 0.023%, and 0.091% in the Americas.

The share of imports in GDP of Greenland was 94.2% in the 1980s, ranked 11th in the world, and was on a par with the Cook Islands (94.2%), Macao (94.8%).

The Greenland's imports per capita were $11 201.7 in the 1980s, ranked 6th in the world, and were on a par with Monaco ($10.9 thousand). The Greenland's imports per capita were greater than imports per capita in the world ($539.1) in 20.8 times, and were greater than imports per capita in the Americas ($984.9) in 11.4 times.

The growth of imports in Greenland was -1.2% in the 1980s, ranked 156th in the world. The growth of imports in Greenland (-1.2%) was less than growth of imports in the world (3.8%), was less than growth of imports in the Americas (3.8%).

Comparison with neighbors. The Greenland's imports were less than in Canada ($94.9 billion) and in Iceland ($1.4 billion). The Greenland's imports per capita were greater than in Iceland ($5.8 thousand) and in Canada ($3.7 thousand). The growth of imports in Greenland was less than in Canada (4.6%) and in Iceland (2.3%).

Comparison with leaders. The Greenland's imports were less than in the USA ($417.2 billion), in Germany ($225.6 billion), in Japan

($175.9 billion), in France ($162.0 billion), and in the UK ($157.7 billion). The imports per capita in Greenland were greater than in Germany ($2.9 thousand), in France ($2.9 thousand), in the United Kingdom ($2.8 thousand), in the USA ($1 742.4), and in Japan ($1 450.4). The growth of imports in Greenland was less than in the United States (5.8%), in the United Kingdom (5.1%), in Japan (4.6%), in France (4.3%), and in Germany (3.3%).

The 1990s

The value of imports in Greenland was $693.8 million per year in the 1990s, ranked 158th in the world, and was on a par with Malawi ($696.5 million), Togo ($690.3 million). The share in the world was 0.012%, and 0.050% in the Americas.

The share of imports in GDP of Greenland was 59.0% in the 1990s, ranked 46th in the world, and was on a par with the Solomon Islands (59.1%), the TCI (58.8%), Belize (58.8%).

The Greenland's imports per capita were $12 423.9 in the 1990s, ranked 14th in the world. The imports per capita in Greenland were greater than imports per capita in the world ($1 015.5) in 12.2 times, and were greater than imports per capita in the Americas ($1 812.7) in 6.9 times.

The growth of imports in Greenland was -1.9% in the 1990s, ranked 178th in the world, and was on a par with Iran (-1.9%). The growth of imports in Greenland (-1.9%) was less than growth of imports in the world (6.6%), was less than growth of imports in the Americas (8.2%).

Comparison with neighbors. The imports of Greenland were less than in Canada ($195.7 billion) and in Iceland ($2.4 billion). The Greenland's imports per capita were greater than in Iceland ($9.1 thousand) and in Canada ($6.8 thousand). The growth of imports in Greenland was less than in Canada (6.4%) and in Iceland (4.4%).

Comparison with leaders. The value of imports in Greenland was less than in the USA ($874.1 billion), in Germany ($501.6 billion), in Japan ($355.9 billion), in the United Kingdom ($330.2 billion), and in France ($308.5 billion). The imports per capita in Greenland were greater than in Germany ($6.2 thousand), in the UK ($5.7 thousand), in France ($5.2 thousand), in the USA ($3.3 thousand), and in Japan ($2.8 thousand). The growth of imports in Greenland was less than in the USA (8.3%), in Germany (6.4%), in France (5.1%), in the UK (5.1%), and in Japan (3.3%).

The 2000s

The imports of Greenland were $1.0 billion per year in the 2000s, ranked 169th in the world. The share in the world was 0.0081%, and 0.034% in the Americas.

The structure of imports: primary products (8.1%), resource-based manufactures (35.8%), low technology manufactures (18.1%), medium technology manufactures (23.8%), and high technology manufactures (11.4%).

Greenland imported goods from Denmark (71.2%), Sweden (13.1%), Norway (4.9%), Canada (1.9%), Iceland (1.3%) and other countries (7.7%).

The share of imports in GDP of Greenland was 55.5% in the 2000s, ranked 69th in the world, and was on a par with the Solomon Islands (55.2%), Papua New Guinea (55.8%).

The Greenlandic imports per capita were $17 757.4 in the 2000s, ranked 21st in the world, and were on a par with Norway ($17.9 thousand). The imports per capita in Greenland were greater than imports per capita in the world ($1 899.9) in 9.3 times, and were greater than imports per capita in the Americas ($3 354.4) in 5.3 times.

The growth of imports in Greenland was 2% in the 2000s, ranked 175th in the world, and was on a par with Israel (2.0%). The growth of imports in Greenland (2.0%) was less than growth of imports in the world (5.1%), was less than growth of imports in the Americas (3.5%).

Comparison with neighbors. The imports of Greenland were less than in Canada ($366.5 billion) and in Iceland ($5.6 billion). The imports per capita in Greenland were greater than in Canada ($11.4 thousand); but less than in Iceland ($19.1 thousand). The growth of imports in Greenland was greater than in Iceland (0.12%); but less than in Canada (2.3%).

Comparison with leaders. The value of imports in Greenland was less than in the USA ($1.9 trillion), in Germany ($914.7 billion), in the United Kingdom ($641.8 billion), in China ($641.1 billion), and in Japan ($566.4 billion). The Greenlandic imports per capita were greater than in Germany ($11.2 thousand), in the United Kingdom ($10.6 thousand), in the United States ($6.4 thousand), in Japan

($4.4 thousand), and in China ($483.3). The growth of imports in Greenland was greater than in Japan (1.8%); but less than in China (15.1%), in Germany (3.7%), in the United Kingdom (3.1%), and in the USA (2.8%).

The 2010s

The Greenland's imports were $1.5 billion per year in the 2010s, ranked 174th in the world. The share in the world was 0.0069%, and 0.032% in the Americas.

The structure of imports: primary products (8.4%), resource-based manufactures (35.8%), low technology manufactures (17.8%), medium technology manufactures (22.9%), and high technology manufactures (11.4%).

Greenland imported goods from Denmark (62.7%), Sweden (16.7%), Iceland (3.8%), the United Kingdom (3.0%), Norway (2.1%) and other countries (11.6%).

The share of imports in GDP of Greenland was 55.9% in the 2010s, ranked 67th in the world, and was on a par with Vanuatu (55.7%), Antigua and Barbuda (55.6%), the TCI (55.6%).

The imports per capita in Greenland were $27 124.0 in the 2010s, ranked 17th in the world, and were on a par with the UAE ($27.7 thousand), Sint Maarten ($27.7 thousand). The value of imports per capita in Greenland was greater than imports per capita in the world ($3 015.6) in 9.0 times, and was greater than imports per capita in the Americas ($4 884.3) in 5.6 times.

The growth of imports in Greenland was 1.3% in the 2010s, ranked 175th in the world. The growth of imports in Greenland (1.3%) was less than growth of imports in the world (4.4%), was less than growth of imports in the Americas (3.3%).

Comparison with neighbors. The Greenland's imports were 366.7 times lower than in Canada ($562.0 billion) and 5.4 times lower than in Iceland ($8.3 billion). The imports per capita in Greenland were 7.2% higher than in Iceland ($25.3 thousand) and 72.9% higher than in Canada ($15.7 thousand). The growth of imports in Greenland was less than in Iceland (5.5%) and in Canada (3.6%).

Comparison with leaders. The Greenland's imports were 1 838.4 times lower than in the USA ($2.8 trillion), 1 350.2 times lower than in China ($2.1 trillion), 949.3 times lower than in Germany ($1.5 trillion), 572.9 times lower than in Japan ($877.9 billion), and 557.8 times lower than in the UK ($854.8 billion). The value of imports per capita in Greenland was 52.6% higher than in Germany ($17.8 thousand), 2.1 times higher than in the UK ($13.0 thousand), 3.1 times higher than in the USA ($8.8 thousand), 4.0 times higher than in Japan ($6.9 thousand), and 18.4 times higher than in China ($1 475.4). The growth of imports in Greenland was less than in China (8.2%), in Germany (4.8%), in the United States (4.4%), in Japan (3.8%), and in the United Kingdom (3.6%).

Part IV. Consumption

Chapter XII. Government consumption expenditure

General government final consumption expenditure

The government consumption expenditure of Greenland rose from $52.4 million per year in the 1970s to $1.2 billion per year in the 2010s, that is by $1.2 billion or 23.5 times. The change occurred at $994.7 million due to a 5.2-fold increase in prices, as also at $177.5 million due to a 3.9-fold increase in per capita rate, as well as at $8.2 million due to the growth in population. The average annual growth in government expenditure is 3.7%. The minimum value of government consumption expenditure was in 1970 at $19.4 million. The maximum value of government consumption expenditure was in 2018 at $1.3 billion.

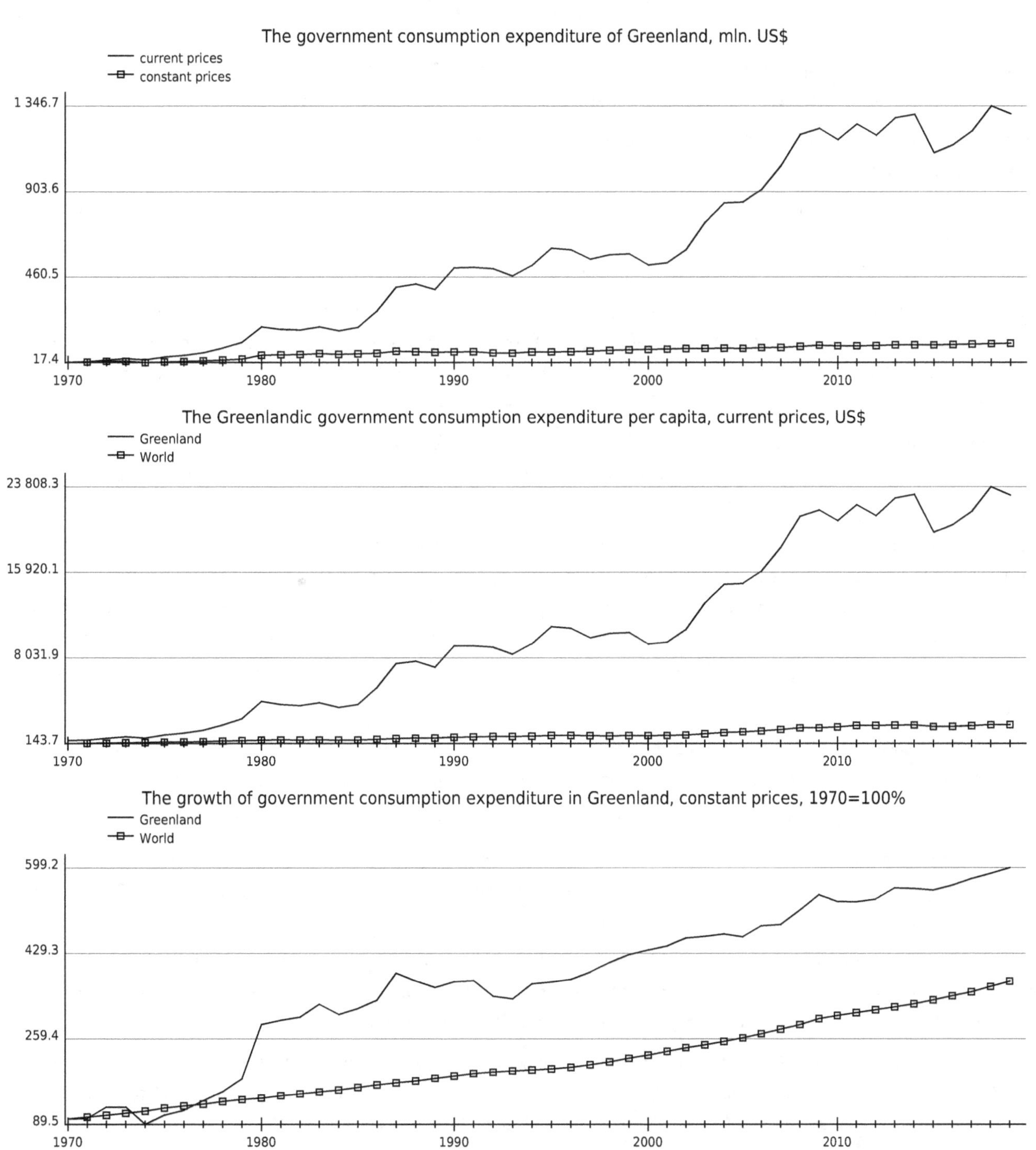

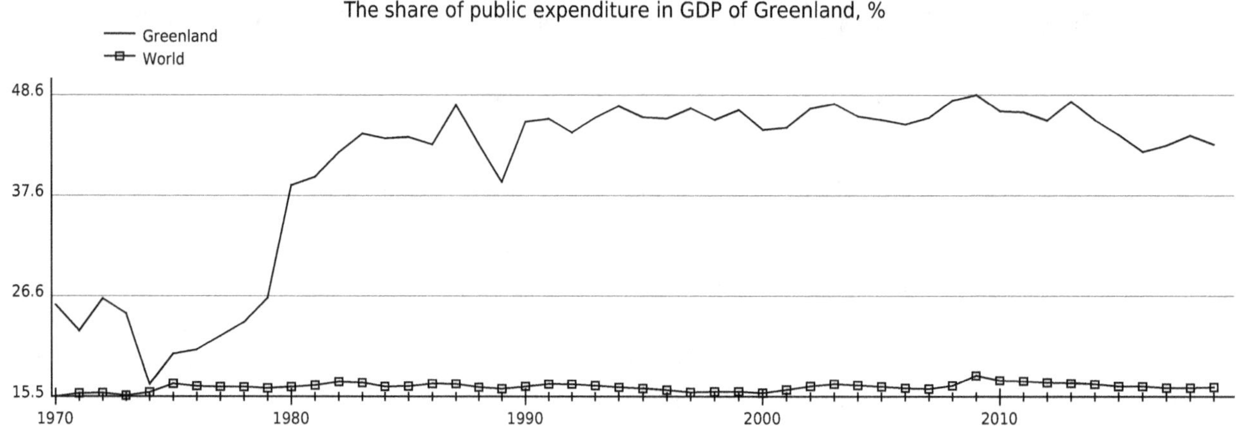

The 1970s

The Greenland's government expenditure was $52.4 million per year in the 1970s, ranked 142nd in the world, and was on a par with Botswana ($52.7 million), Burundi ($51.8 million). The share in the world was 0.0049%, and 0.014% in the Americas.

The share of government consumption expenditure in GDP of Greenland was 23.0% in the 1970s, ranked 28th in the world, and was on a par with the Solomon Islands (23.0%).

The Greenland's government expenditure per capita was $1 073.6 in the 1970s, ranked 24th in the world, and was on a par with Northern Europe ($1 066.0). The public expenditure per capita in Greenland was greater than government consumption expenditure per capita in the world ($265.2) in 4.0 times, and was greater than public expenditure per capita in the Americas ($655.5) by 63.8%.

The growth of government consumption expenditure in Greenland was 6.8% in the 1970s, ranked 70th in the world, and was on a par with Ethiopia (6.7%), Western Africa (6.8%), Yugoslav SFR (6.8%). The growth of government expenditure in Greenland (6.8%) was greater than growth of government consumption expenditure in the world (3.7%), was greater than growth of government expenditure in the Americas (2.1%).

Comparison with neighbors. The government expenditure of Greenland was less than in Canada ($35.9 billion) and in Iceland ($249.5 million). The public expenditure per capita in Greenland was less than in Canada ($1 570.5) and in Iceland ($1 154.8). The growth of public expenditure in Greenland was greater than in Canada (3.4%); but less than in Iceland (7.5%).

Comparison with leaders. The government consumption expenditure of Greenland was less than in the United States ($285.9 billion), in the USSR ($117.3 billion), in Germany ($95.6 billion), in Japan ($78.0 billion), and in France ($64.5 billion). The Greenland's government expenditure per capita was greater than in Japan ($700.2) and in the USSR ($465.0); but less than in the USA ($1 310.2), in Germany ($1 213.7), and in France ($1 202.3). The growth of government expenditure in Greenland was greater than in Japan (5.3%), in France (5.0%), in Germany (4.4%), and in the USA (0.94%); but less than in the USSR (7.2%).

The 1980s

The Greenland's public expenditure was $267.2 million per year in the 1980s, ranked 122nd in the world, and was on a par with Palestine ($267.1 million), Malawi ($272.5 million). The share in the world was 0.011%, and 0.031% in the Americas.

The share of government expenditure in GDP of Greenland was 42.6% in the 1980s, ranked 6th in the world.

The government expenditure per capita in Greenland was $5 062.0 in the 1980s, ranked 3rd in the world. The Greenlandic government expenditure per capita was greater than government consumption expenditure per capita in the world ($523.5) in 9.7 times, and was greater than government consumption expenditure per capita in the Americas ($1 287.2) in 3.9 times.

The growth of government expenditure in Greenland was 7.2% in the 1980s, ranked 20th in the world, and was on a par with Zimbabwe (7.1%). The growth of government consumption expenditure in Greenland (7.2%) was greater than growth of government expenditure in the world (2.7%), was greater than growth of government expenditure in the Americas (2.5%).

Comparison with neighbors. The Greenlandic public expenditure was less than in Canada ($84.0 billion) and in Iceland ($735.5 million). The Greenlandic public expenditure per capita was greater than in Canada ($3.3 thousand) and in Iceland ($3.1 thousand). The growth of public expenditure in Greenland was greater than in Iceland (4.9%) and in Canada (2.1%).

Comparison with leaders. The Greenlandic public expenditure was less than in the USA ($665.3 billion), in Japan ($257.4 billion), in Germany ($203.7 billion), in the USSR ($181.1 billion), and in France ($159.8 billion). The Greenland's public expenditure per capita was greater than in France ($2.8 thousand), in the United States ($2.8 thousand), in Germany ($2.6 thousand), in Japan ($2.1 thousand), and in the USSR ($658.0). The growth of government expenditure in Greenland was greater than in the USSR (5.4%), in Japan (3.5%), in France (2.8%), in the USA (2.6%), and in Germany (0.98%).

The 1990s

The government consumption expenditure of Greenland was $543.1 million per year in the 1990s, ranked 130th in the world, and was on a par with the Bahamas ($545.1 million), Niger ($554.7 million). The share in the world was 0.012%, and 0.036% in the Americas.

The share of government expenditure in GDP of Greenland was 46.2% in the 1990s, ranked 5th in the world, and was on a par with Micronesia (46.1%).

The government expenditure per capita in Greenland was $9 725.1 in the 1990s, ranked 2nd in the world. The government expenditure per capita in Greenland was greater than public expenditure per capita in the world ($824.8) in 11.8 times, and was greater than public expenditure per capita in the Americas ($1 972.7) in 4.9 times.

The growth of government expenditure in Greenland was 1.7% in the 1990s, ranked 122nd in the world, and was on a par with Panama (1.7%). The growth of government expenditure in Greenland (1.7%) was less than growth of government expenditure in the world (2.0%), was greater than growth of public expenditure in the Americas (1.1%).

Comparison with neighbors. The Greenland's government consumption expenditure was less than in Canada ($134.6 billion) and in Iceland ($1.5 billion). The public expenditure per capita in Greenland was greater than in Iceland ($5.7 thousand) and in Canada ($4.6 thousand). The growth of government expenditure in Greenland was greater than in Canada (0.56%); but less than in Iceland (2.8%).

Comparison with leaders. The Greenlandic public expenditure was less than in the USA ($1.1 trillion), in Japan ($651.8 billion), in Germany ($419.6 billion), in France ($325.4 billion), and in the United Kingdom ($234.6 billion). The Greenland's government consumption expenditure per capita was greater than in France ($5.5 thousand), in Germany ($5.2 thousand), in Japan ($5.2 thousand), in the USA ($4.3 thousand), and in the United Kingdom ($4.1 thousand). The growth of public expenditure in Greenland was greater than in the United States (1.3%); but less than in Japan (3.0%), in Germany (2.4%), in the United Kingdom (2.1%), and in France (1.8%).

The 2000s

The government consumption expenditure of Greenland was $847.2 million per year in the 2000s, ranked 134th in the world, and was on a par with Albania ($828.9 million). The share in the world was 0.011%, and 0.033% in the Americas.

The share of government consumption expenditure in GDP of Greenland was 46.7% in the 2000s, ranked 6th in the world.

The Greenland's government consumption expenditure per capita was $14 940.9 in the 2000s, ranked 2nd in the world. The government expenditure per capita in Greenland was greater than government expenditure per capita in the world ($1 200.9) in 12.4 times, and was greater than public expenditure per capita in the Americas ($2 931.6) in 5.1 times.

The growth of public expenditure in Greenland was 2.5% in the 2000s, ranked 139th in the world, and was on a par with Nicaragua (2.5%), the Marshall Islands (2.5%), Norway (2.5%). The growth of government expenditure in Greenland (2.5%) was less than growth of government consumption expenditure in the world (3.1%), was greater than growth of public expenditure in the Americas (2.4%).

Comparison with neighbors. The government consumption expenditure of Greenland was less than in Canada ($218.3 billion) and in Iceland ($3.3 billion). The Greenland's government expenditure per capita was greater than in Iceland ($11.1 thousand) and in Canada ($6.8 thousand). The growth of government consumption expenditure in Greenland was less than in Iceland (3.6%) and in Canada (2.6%).

Comparison with leaders. The Greenland's government consumption expenditure was less than in the United States ($1.9 trillion), in Japan ($844.2 billion), in Germany ($520.1 billion), in France ($479.9 billion), and in the UK ($453.4 billion). The Greenlandic government expenditure per capita was greater than in France ($7.6 thousand), in the UK ($7.5 thousand), in Japan ($6.6 thousand), in the United States ($6.5 thousand), and in Germany ($6.4 thousand). The growth of government consumption expenditure in Greenland was greater than in the United States (2.2%), in Japan (1.7%), in France (1.7%), and in Germany (1.4%); but less than in the United Kingdom (2.9%).

The 2010s

The public expenditure of Greenland was $1.2 billion per year in the 2010s, ranked 148th in the world, and was on a par with Kyrgyzstan ($1.3 billion). The share in the world was 0.0094%, and 0.031% in the Americas.

The share of government consumption expenditure in GDP of Greenland was 44.9% in the 2010s, ranked 6th in the world.

The Greenlandic government consumption expenditure per capita was $21 820.6 in the 2010s, ranked 2nd in the world. The Greenlandic public expenditure per capita was greater than government consumption expenditure per capita in the world ($1 785.1) in 12.2 times, and was greater than government expenditure per capita in the Americas ($4 034.3) in 5.4 times.

The growth of government consumption expenditure in Greenland was 0.9% in the 2010s, ranked 151st in the world, and was on a par with Suriname (0.96%). The growth of public expenditure in Greenland (0.95%) was less than growth of government expenditure in the world (2.3%), was greater than growth of government consumption expenditure in the Americas (0.45%).

Comparison with neighbors. The Greenland's public expenditure was 290.0 times lower than in Canada ($357.5 billion) and 3.7 times lower than in Iceland ($4.5 billion). The government consumption expenditure per capita in Greenland was 58.4% higher than in Iceland ($13.8 thousand) and 2.2 times higher than in Canada ($10.0 thousand). The growth of government expenditure in Greenland was less than in Canada (1.4%) and in Iceland (1.1%).

Comparison with leaders. The Greenlandic public expenditure was 2 152.3 times lower than in the USA ($2.7 trillion), 1 362.0 times lower than in China ($1.7 trillion), 846.0 times lower than in Japan ($1.0 trillion), 585.3 times lower than in Germany ($721.6 billion), and 517.4 times lower than in France ($637.9 billion). The Greenland's government consumption expenditure per capita was 2.3 times higher than in France ($9.6 thousand), 2.5 times higher than in Germany ($8.8 thousand), 2.6 times higher than in the United States ($8.3 thousand), 2.7 times higher than in Japan ($8.2 thousand), and 18.2 times higher than in China ($1 197.3). The growth of government consumption expenditure in Greenland was greater than in the United States (0.0052%); but less than in China (8.3%), in Germany (1.9%), in Japan (1.3%), and in France (1.3%).

Chapter XIII. Household consumption expenditure

(including Non-profit institutions serving households)

The household expenditure of Greenland rose from $178.3 million per year in the 1970s to $1.1 billion per year in the 2010s, that is by $913.5 million or 6.1 times. The change occurred at $874.8 million due to a 5.0-fold increase in prices, as also at $10.8 million due to a 1.1-fold increase in per capita rate, as well as at $28.0 million due to the growth in population. The average annual growth in household expenditure is 0.45%. The minimum value of household expenditure was in 1970 at $86.0 million. The maximum value of household expenditure was in 2014 at $1.2 billion.

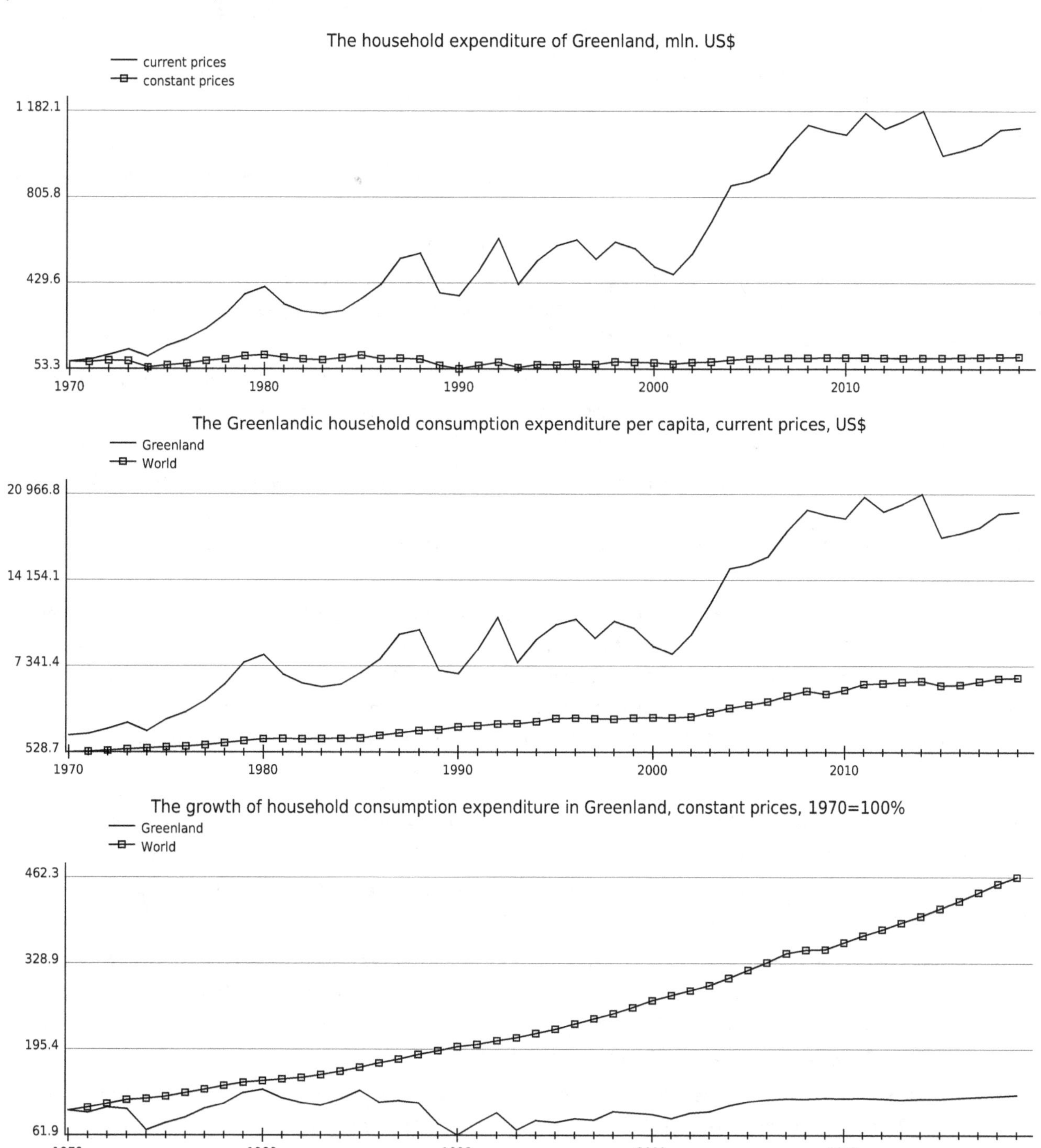

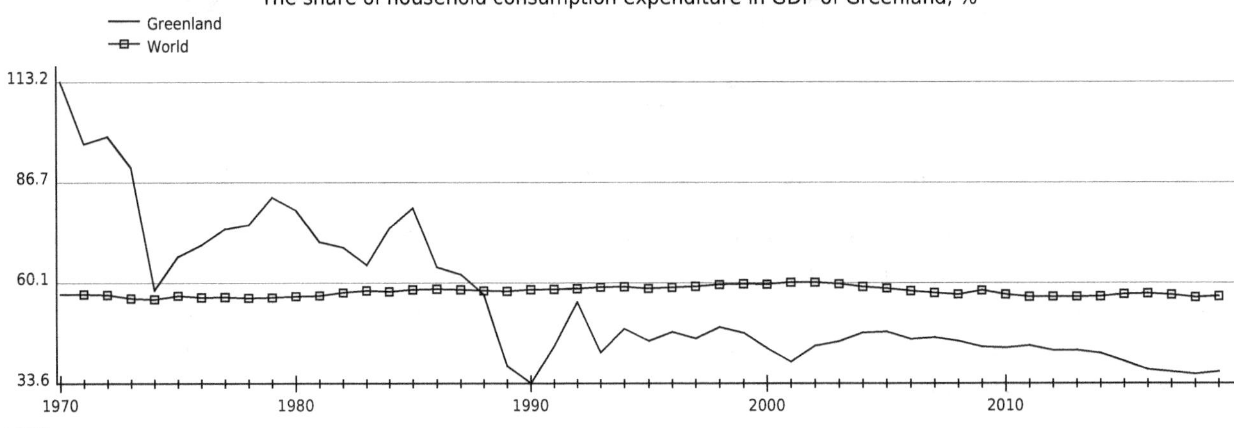

The 1970s

The Greenland's household expenditure was $178.3 million per year in the 1970s, ranked 148th in the world, and was on a par with Liechtenstein ($178.8 million), Laos ($177.4 million), Botswana ($180.6 million). The share in the world was 0.0048%, and 0.013% in the Americas.

The share of household expenditure in GDP of Greenland was 78.3% in the 1970s, ranked 39th in the world, and was on a par with Colombia (78.1%), Puerto Rico (78.4%), India (77.8%).

The Greenland's household expenditure per capita was $3 651.4 in the 1970s, ranked 18th in the world, and was on a par with Australasia ($3.7 thousand), the Netherlands ($3.7 thousand). The household consumption expenditure per capita in Greenland was greater than household expenditure per capita in the world ($914.8) in 4.0 times, and was greater than household consumption expenditure per capita in the Americas ($2 467.5) by 48.0%.

The growth of household expenditure in Greenland was 2.8% in the 1970s, ranked 141st in the world. The growth of household consumption expenditure in Greenland (2.8%) was less than growth of household consumption expenditure in the world (4.1%), was less than growth of household expenditure in the Americas (4.1%).

Comparison with neighbors. The household consumption expenditure of Greenland was less than in Canada ($90.2 billion) and in Iceland ($867.8 million). The Greenlandic household expenditure per capita was less than in Iceland ($4.0 thousand) and in Canada ($4.0 thousand). The growth of household consumption expenditure in Greenland was less than in Iceland (6.5%) and in Canada (4.6%).

Comparison with leaders. The household expenditure of Greenland was less than in the United States ($1.0 trillion), in the USSR ($310.6 billion), in Japan ($280.9 billion), in Germany ($277.8 billion), and in France ($180.7 billion). The household expenditure per capita in Greenland was greater than in Germany ($3.5 thousand), in France ($3.4 thousand), in Japan ($2.5 thousand), and in the USSR ($1 231.6); but less than in the United States ($4.7 thousand). The growth of household consumption expenditure in Greenland was less than in Japan (5.1%), in the USSR (4.7%), in France (4.0%), in the United States (3.6%), and in Germany (3.6%).

The 1980s

The Greenland's household expenditure was $392.7 million per year in the 1980s, ranked 150th in the world, and was on a par with Andorra ($386.3 million), Guinea-Bissau ($401.3 million). The share in the world was 0.0045%, and 0.012% in the Americas.

The share of household consumption expenditure in GDP of Greenland was 62.6% in the 1980s, ranked 99th in the world, and was on a par with the USA (62.6%), the Solomon Islands (62.6%), the Americas (62.3%).

The Greenland's household consumption expenditure per capita was $7 439.2 in the 1980s, ranked 19th in the world, and was on a par with Western Europe ($7.4 thousand), Australasia ($7.4 thousand), Germany ($7.4 thousand). The Greenland's household consumption expenditure per capita was greater than household expenditure per capita in the world ($1 808.0) in 4.1 times, and was greater than household expenditure per capita in the Americas ($5 090.2) by 46.1%.

The growth of household expenditure in Greenland was -4.6% in the 1980s, ranked 184th in the world. The growth of household consumption expenditure in Greenland (-4.6%) was less than growth of household consumption expenditure in the world (3.0%), was less than growth of household consumption expenditure in the Americas (2.9%).

Comparison with neighbors. The household consumption expenditure of Greenland was less than in Canada ($209.0 billion) and in Iceland ($2.4 billion). The Greenland's household consumption expenditure per capita was less than in Iceland ($10.0 thousand) and in Canada ($8.1 thousand). The growth of household consumption expenditure in Greenland was less than in Iceland (3.0%) and in Canada (2.6%).

Comparison with leaders. The household expenditure of Greenland was less than in the USA ($2.6 trillion), in Japan ($945.6 billion), in Germany ($575.7 billion), in the USSR ($424.6 billion), and in the UK ($416.5 billion). The Greenland's household expenditure per capita was greater than in Germany ($7.4 thousand), in the UK ($7.4 thousand), and in the USSR ($1 542.8); but less than in the USA ($10.9 thousand) and in Japan ($7.8 thousand). The growth of household consumption expenditure in Greenland was less than in Japan (3.7%), in the United Kingdom (3.5%), in the United States (3.2%), in the USSR (3.0%), and in Germany (1.8%).

The 1990s

The Greenland's household expenditure was $536.6 million per year in the 1990s, ranked 175th in the world, and was on a par with Saint Lucia ($537.6 million), Guyana ($537.8 million), Eritrea ($545.7 million). The share in the world was 0.0032%, and 0.0083% in the Americas.

The share of household consumption expenditure in GDP of Greenland was 45.6% in the 1990s, ranked 191st in the world, and was on a par with the Cook Islands (45.9%), China (46.0%).

The Greenland's household expenditure per capita was $9 608.7 in the 1990s, ranked 32nd in the world, and was on a par with the Virgin Islands ($9.6 thousand), French Polynesia ($9.6 thousand), Aruba ($9.5 thousand). The Greenlandic household expenditure per capita was greater than household expenditure per capita in the world ($2 963.9) in 3.2 times, and was greater than household expenditure per capita in the Americas ($8 394.4) by 14.5%.

The growth of household expenditure in Greenland was 1.9% in the 1990s, ranked 134th in the world. The growth of household expenditure in Greenland (1.9%) was less than growth of household consumption expenditure in the world (3.0%), was less than growth of household consumption expenditure in the Americas (3.3%).

Comparison with neighbors. The household expenditure of Greenland was less than in Canada ($349.9 billion) and in Iceland ($4.2 billion). The Greenlandic household consumption expenditure per capita was less than in Iceland ($15.9 thousand) and in Canada ($12.1 thousand). The growth of household expenditure in Greenland was less than in Iceland (2.5%) and in Canada (2.3%).

Comparison with leaders. The Greenland's household expenditure was less than in the USA ($4.9 trillion), in Japan ($2.3 trillion), in Germany ($1.2 trillion), in the UK ($884.5 billion), and in France ($783.0 billion). The household consumption expenditure per capita in Greenland was less than in the USA ($18.5 thousand), in Japan ($18.2 thousand), in the United Kingdom ($15.3 thousand), in Germany ($15.2 thousand), and in France ($13.2 thousand). The growth of household expenditure in Greenland was greater than in Japan (1.8%) and in France (1.8%); but less than in the USA (3.4%), in the United Kingdom (2.8%), and in Germany (2.1%).

The 2000s

The household expenditure of Greenland was $811.3 million per year in the 2000s, ranked 176th in the world, and was on a par with Eritrea ($800.1 million). The share in the world was 0.0030%, and 0.0074% in the Americas.

The share of household expenditure in GDP of Greenland was 44.7% in the 2000s, ranked 182nd in the world.

The Greenland's household expenditure per capita was $14 308.4 in the 2000s, ranked 35th in the world, and was on a par with Oceania ($14.3 thousand), Spain ($14.5 thousand), Greece ($14.1 thousand). The Greenlandic household consumption expenditure per capita was greater than household consumption expenditure per capita in the world ($4 208.2) in 3.4 times, and was greater than household expenditure per capita in the Americas ($12 522.4) by 14.3%.

The growth of household consumption expenditure in Greenland was 2.2% in the 2000s, ranked 164th in the world. The growth of household consumption expenditure in Greenland (2.2%) was less than growth of household expenditure in the world (3.0%), was less than growth of household consumption expenditure in the Americas (2.7%).

Comparison with neighbors. The household consumption expenditure of Greenland was less than in Canada ($609.6 billion) and in Iceland ($7.7 billion). The Greenlandic household consumption expenditure per capita was less than in Iceland ($26.1 thousand) and in Canada ($19.0 thousand). The growth of household expenditure in Greenland was greater than in Iceland (1.4%); but less than in Canada (3.2%).

Comparison with leaders. The Greenland's household consumption expenditure was less than in the USA ($8.5 trillion), in Japan ($2.6 trillion), in Germany ($1.5 trillion), in the United Kingdom ($1.5 trillion), and in France ($1.1 trillion). The household consumption expenditure per capita in Greenland was less than in the United States ($28.8 thousand), in the UK ($25.0 thousand), in Japan ($20.4 thousand), in Germany ($18.9 thousand), and in France ($18.1 thousand). The growth of household consumption expenditure in Greenland was greater than in the United Kingdom (2.1%), in France (2.0%), in Japan (0.81%), and in Germany (0.46%); but less than in the USA (2.4%).

The 2010s

The Greenlandic household consumption expenditure was $1.1 billion per year in the 2010s, ranked 181st in the world, and was on a par with Somalia ($1.1 billion). The share in the world was 0.0025%, and 0.0064% in the Americas.

The share of household consumption expenditure in GDP of Greenland was 39.8% in the 2010s, ranked 188th in the world.

The household consumption expenditure per capita in Greenland was $19 325.9 in the 2010s, ranked 32nd in the world, and was on a par with the Bahamas ($19.4 thousand), San Marino ($19.8 thousand). The household consumption expenditure per capita in Greenland was greater than household consumption expenditure per capita in the world ($6 018.5) in 3.2 times, and was greater than household expenditure per capita in the Americas ($17 389.9) by 11.1%.

The growth of household consumption expenditure in Greenland was 0.4% in the 2010s, ranked 188th in the world. The growth of household consumption expenditure in Greenland (0.40%) was less than growth of household expenditure in the world (2.8%), was less than growth of household consumption expenditure in the Americas (2.2%).

Comparison with neighbors. The household consumption expenditure of Greenland was 892.2 times lower than in Canada ($974.2 billion) and 8.9 times lower than in Iceland ($9.7 billion). The Greenlandic household expenditure per capita was 34.5% lower than in Iceland ($29.5 thousand) and 28.9% lower than in Canada ($27.2 thousand). The growth of household expenditure in Greenland was less than in Iceland (3.4%) and in Canada (2.5%).

Comparison with leaders. The Greenland's household expenditure was 11 166.5 times lower than in the United States ($12.2 trillion), 3 598.9 times lower than in China ($3.9 trillion), 2 736.1 times lower than in Japan ($3.0 trillion), 1 793.7 times lower than in Germany ($2.0 trillion), and 1 632.1 times lower than in the United Kingdom ($1.8 trillion). The household consumption expenditure per capita in Greenland was 6.9 times higher than in China ($2.8 thousand); but 49.4% lower than in the United States ($38.2 thousand), 28.9% lower than in the United Kingdom ($27.2 thousand), 19.2% lower than in Germany ($23.9 thousand), and 17.2% lower than in Japan ($23.4 thousand). The growth of household consumption expenditure in Greenland was less than in China (8.3%), in the USA (2.4%), in the United Kingdom (1.8%), in Germany (1.4%), and in Japan (0.64%).

Part V. Reproduction

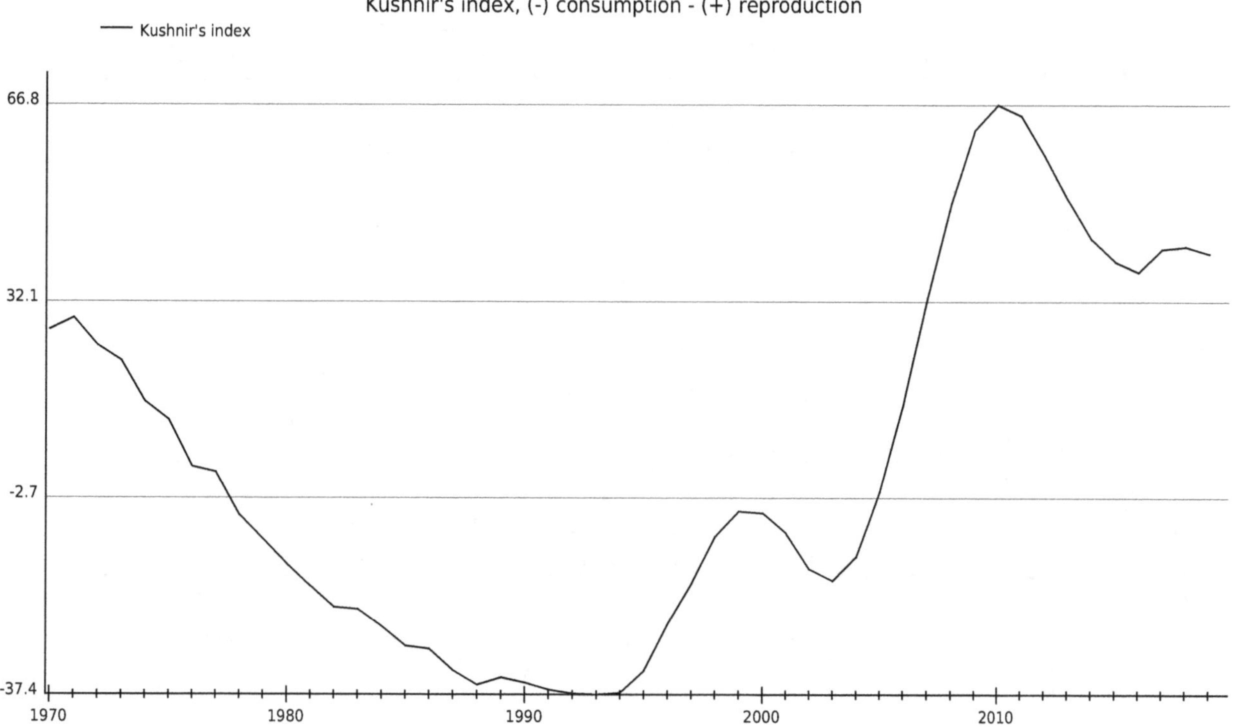

Chapter XIV. Gross fixed capital formation

(including Acquisitions less disposals of valuables)

The fixed capital formation of Greenland enlarged from $89.8 million per year in the 1970s to $890.9 million per year in the 2010s, that is by $801.2 million or 9.9 times. The change occurred at $705.6 million due to a 4.8-fold increase in prices, as also at $81.5 million due to a 1.8-fold increase in per capita rate, as well as at $14.1 million due to the expansion in population. The average annual growth in fixed capital formation is 1.8%. The minimum value of fixed capital formation was in 1970 at $35.3 million. The maximum value of gross fixed capital formation was in 2011 at $1.7 billion.

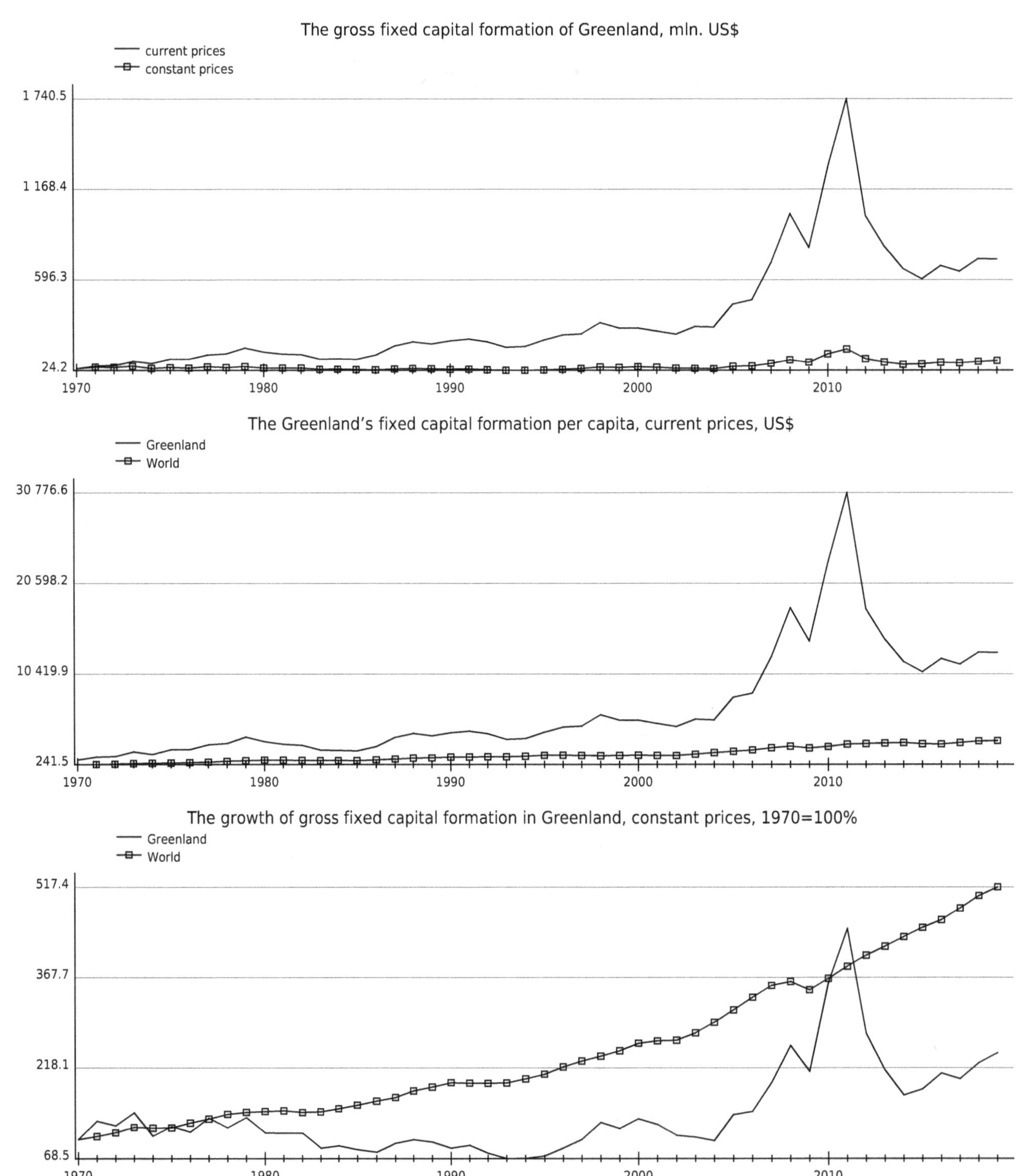

The gross fixed capital formation of Greenland, mln. US$

The Greenland's fixed capital formation per capita, current prices, US$

The growth of gross fixed capital formation in Greenland, constant prices, 1970=100%

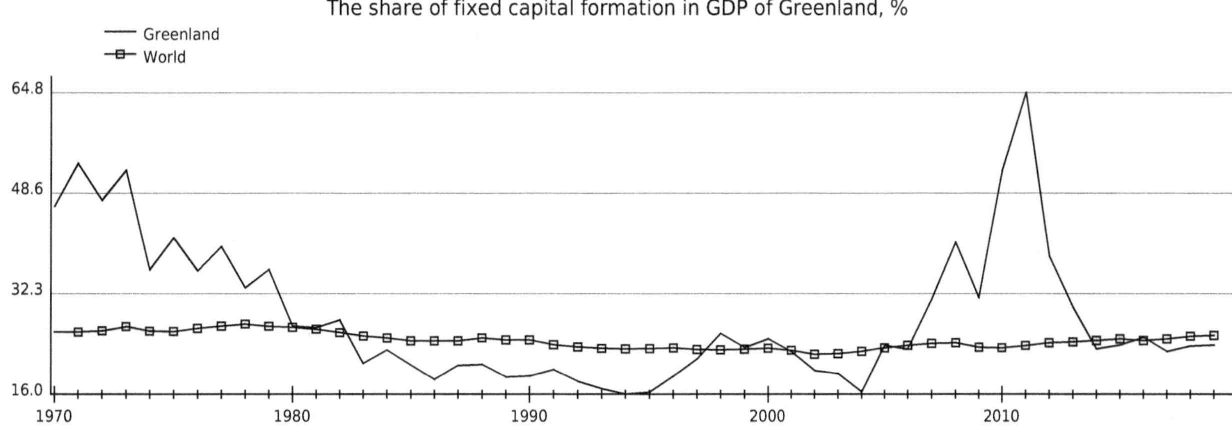

The 1970s

The gross fixed capital formation of Greenland was $89.8 million per year in the 1970s, ranked 136th in the world, and was on a par with Sierra Leone ($90.1 million), Chad ($91.1 million), Macao ($87.6 million). The share in the world was 0.0051%, and 0.018% in the Americas.

The share of fixed capital formation in GDP of Greenland was 39.4% in the 1970s, ranked 11th in the world, and was on a par with Hungary (39.3%), Gabon (39.2%), Algeria (39.7%).

The gross fixed capital formation per capita in Greenland was $1 838.2 in the 1970s, ranked 16th in the world, and was on a par with French Polynesia ($1 839.4), Denmark ($1 849.5). The Greenland's fixed capital formation per capita was greater than fixed capital formation per capita in the world ($433.5) in 4.2 times, and was greater than fixed capital formation per capita in the Americas ($913.4) in 2.0 times.

The growth of fixed capital formation in Greenland was 3.5% in the 1970s, ranked 124th in the world, and was on a par with Djibouti (3.5%). The growth of gross fixed capital formation in Greenland (3.5%) was less than growth of fixed capital formation in the world (4.2%), was less than growth of gross fixed capital formation in the Americas (5.3%).

Comparison with neighbors. The Greenlandic fixed capital formation was less than in Canada ($38.6 billion) and in Iceland ($495.3 million). The fixed capital formation per capita in Greenland was greater than in Canada ($1 687.5); but less than in Iceland ($2.3 thousand). The growth of gross fixed capital formation in Greenland was less than in Iceland (6.4%) and in Canada (5.1%).

Comparison with leaders. The Greenlandic gross fixed capital formation was less than in the USA ($381.9 billion), in the USSR ($214.6 billion), in Japan ($191.6 billion), in Germany ($125.8 billion), and in France ($82.9 billion). The Greenlandic gross fixed capital formation per capita was greater than in the United States ($1 750.0), in Japan ($1 720.7), in Germany ($1 597.2), in France ($1 545.4), and in the USSR ($850.9). The growth of fixed capital formation in Greenland was greater than in the USSR (3.2%), in France (2.7%), and in Germany (1.5%); but less than in the USA (4.4%) and in Japan (3.9%).

The 1980s

The gross fixed capital formation of Greenland was $137.2 million per year in the 1980s, ranked 144th in the world, and was on a par with Aruba ($138.5 million), Andorra ($138.8 million). The share in the world was 0.0036%, and 0.011% in the Americas.

The share of gross fixed capital formation in GDP of Greenland was 21.9% in the 1980s, ranked 96th in the world, and was on a par with Melanesia (21.8%), South America (21.8%), Sri Lanka (22.0%).

The gross fixed capital formation per capita in Greenland was $2 599.9 in the 1980s, ranked 28th in the world. The fixed capital formation per capita in Greenland was greater than fixed capital formation per capita in the world ($790.9) in 3.3 times, and was greater than fixed capital formation per capita in the Americas ($1 848.1) by 40.7%.

The growth of gross fixed capital formation in Greenland was -3.5% in the 1980s, ranked 161st in the world. The growth of gross fixed capital formation in Greenland (-3.5%) was less than growth of fixed capital formation in the world (2.5%), was less than growth of gross fixed capital formation in the Americas (1.9%).

Comparison with neighbors. The fixed capital formation of Greenland was less than in Canada ($85.3 billion) and in Iceland ($981.8

million). The Greenland's fixed capital formation per capita was less than in Iceland ($4.1 thousand) and in Canada ($3.3 thousand). The growth of fixed capital formation in Greenland was less than in Canada (3.9%) and in Iceland (1.8%).

Comparison with leaders. The Greenland's gross fixed capital formation was less than in the USA ($958.4 billion), in Japan ($571.7 billion), in the USSR ($271.0 billion), in Germany ($238.1 billion), and in France ($164.3 billion). The Greenlandic fixed capital formation per capita was greater than in the USSR ($984.8); but less than in Japan ($4.7 thousand), in the United States ($4.0 thousand), in Germany ($3.1 thousand), and in France ($2.9 thousand). The growth of gross fixed capital formation in Greenland was less than in Japan (4.8%), in the United States (3.1%), in France (2.4%), in the USSR (1.7%), and in Germany (1.4%).

The 1990s

The gross fixed capital formation of Greenland was $232.2 million per year in the 1990s, ranked 165th in the world. The share in the world was 0.0034%, and 0.011% in the Americas.

The share of fixed capital formation in GDP of Greenland was 19.7% in the 1990s, ranked 138th in the world, and was on a par with Tonga (19.7%), French Polynesia (19.7%), Canada (19.8%).

The gross fixed capital formation per capita in Greenland was $4 158.3 in the 1990s, ranked 34th in the world, and was on a par with Canada ($4.2 thousand), Qatar ($4.3 thousand). The Greenland's gross fixed capital formation per capita was greater than fixed capital formation per capita in the world ($1 183.8) in 3.5 times, and was greater than fixed capital formation per capita in the Americas ($2 694.1) by 54.3%.

The growth of gross fixed capital formation in Greenland was 2.1% in the 1990s, ranked 124th in the world, and was on a par with Gambia (2.1%). The growth of fixed capital formation in Greenland (2.1%) was less than growth of gross fixed capital formation in the world (2.8%), was less than growth of fixed capital formation in the Americas (4.4%).

Comparison with neighbors. The Greenlandic gross fixed capital formation was less than in Canada ($121.9 billion) and in Iceland ($1.5 billion). The fixed capital formation per capita in Greenland was less than in Iceland ($5.8 thousand) and in Canada ($4.2 thousand). The growth of fixed capital formation in Greenland was greater than in Canada (1.8%); but less than in Iceland (3.7%).

Comparison with leaders. The Greenlandic gross fixed capital formation was less than in the USA ($1.6 trillion), in Japan ($1.3 trillion), in Germany ($520.7 billion), in France ($299.3 billion), and in the United Kingdom ($250.0 billion). The fixed capital formation per capita in Greenland was less than in Japan ($10.4 thousand), in Germany ($6.5 thousand), in the United States ($6.1 thousand), in France ($5.0 thousand), and in the UK ($4.3 thousand). The growth of fixed capital formation in Greenland was greater than in the UK (1.7%), in France (1.5%), and in Japan (0.18%); but less than in the USA (4.8%) and in Germany (2.4%).

The 2000s

The Greenlandic fixed capital formation was $484.9 million per year in the 2000s, ranked 165th in the world, and was on a par with Guyana ($489.7 million), Eswatini ($476.1 million). The share in the world was 0.0044%, and 0.014% in the Americas.

The share of gross fixed capital formation in GDP of Greenland was 26.7% in the 2000s, ranked 56th in the world, and was on a par with Algeria (26.7%), São Tomé and Príncipe (26.7%), the Bahamas (26.6%).

The Greenland's fixed capital formation per capita was $8 551.6 in the 2000s, ranked 22nd in the world, and was on a par with Finland ($8.7 thousand), New Caledonia ($8.4 thousand), Austria ($8.7 thousand). The gross fixed capital formation per capita in Greenland was greater than fixed capital formation per capita in the world ($1 690.7) in 5.1 times, and was greater than fixed capital formation per capita in the Americas ($4 079.3) in 2.1 times.

The growth of gross fixed capital formation in Greenland was 6% in the 2000s, ranked 86th in the world, and was on a par with Moldova (6.0%). The growth of fixed capital formation in Greenland (6.0%) was greater than growth of gross fixed capital formation in the world (3.5%), was greater than growth of fixed capital formation in the Americas (1.3%).

Comparison with neighbors. The fixed capital formation of Greenland was less than in Canada ($241.2 billion) and in Iceland ($3.6 billion). The fixed capital formation per capita in Greenland was greater than in Canada ($7.5 thousand); but less than in Iceland ($12.2 thousand). The growth of gross fixed capital formation in Greenland was greater than in Canada (3.2%) and in Iceland (-2.1%).

Comparison with leaders. The gross fixed capital formation of Greenland was less than in the United States ($2.8 trillion), in Japan ($1.2 trillion), in China ($1.0 trillion), in Germany ($557.7 billion), and in France ($463.9 billion). The Greenland's fixed capital formation per capita was greater than in France ($7.4 thousand), in Germany ($6.9 thousand), and in China ($782.2); but less than in the USA ($9.4 thousand) and in Japan ($9.0 thousand). The growth of fixed capital formation in Greenland was greater than in France (1.6%), in the USA (0.43%), in Germany (-0.56%), and in Japan (-2.0%); but less than in China (13.4%).

The 2010s

The Greenlandic fixed capital formation was $890.9 million per year in the 2010s, ranked 162nd in the world, and was on a par with Malawi ($869.7 million). The share in the world was 0.0046%, and 0.017% in the Americas.

The share of gross fixed capital formation in GDP of Greenland was 32.5% in the 2010s, ranked 22nd in the world, and was on a par with Asia (32.3%), Mongolia (32.7%), Indonesia (32.2%).

The Greenlandic fixed capital formation per capita was $15 769.9 in the 2010s, ranked 8th in the world. The gross fixed capital formation per capita in Greenland was greater than fixed capital formation per capita in the world ($2 621.1) in 6.0 times, and was greater than fixed capital formation per capita in the Americas ($5 284.2) in 3.0 times.

The growth of fixed capital formation in Greenland was 1.3% in the 2010s, ranked 146th in the world, and was on a par with Antigua and Barbuda (1.4%). The growth of gross fixed capital formation in Greenland (1.3%) was less than growth of fixed capital formation in the world (4.1%), was less than growth of gross fixed capital formation in the Americas (2.9%).

Comparison with neighbors. The gross fixed capital formation of Greenland was 449.6 times lower than in Canada ($400.6 billion) and 4.0 times lower than in Iceland ($3.6 billion). The gross fixed capital formation per capita in Greenland was 41.0% higher than in Canada ($11.2 thousand) and 45.6% higher than in Iceland ($10.8 thousand). The growth of fixed capital formation in Greenland was less than in Iceland (6.5%) and in Canada (1.9%).

Comparison with leaders. The Greenlandic fixed capital formation was 5 076.3 times lower than in China ($4.5 trillion), 4 039.5 times lower than in the United States ($3.6 trillion), 1 358.3 times lower than in Japan ($1.2 trillion), 844.6 times lower than in Germany ($752.5 billion), and 782.0 times lower than in India ($696.8 billion). The Greenlandic fixed capital formation per capita was 40.0% higher than in the United States ($11.3 thousand), 66.7% higher than in Japan ($9.5 thousand), 71.5% higher than in Germany ($9.2 thousand), 4.9 times higher than in China ($3.2 thousand), and 29.5 times higher than in India ($535.2). The growth of fixed capital formation in Greenland was less than in China (8.0%), in India (5.8%), in the United States (3.8%), in Germany (2.8%), and in Japan (1.8%).